Mad Men Unzipped

Mad Men
Unzipped

Fans on Sex, Love, and the Sixties on TV

Karen E. Dill-Shackleford

Cynthia Vinney

Jerri Lynn Hogg

Kristin Hopper-Losenicky

UNIVERSITY OF IOWA PRESS, IOWA CITY

University of Iowa Press, Iowa City 52242

Copyright © 2015 by the University of Iowa Press

www.uiowapress.org

The University of Iowa Press is a member of Green Press Initiative and
is committed to preserving natural resources.

Printed on acid-free paper

Library of Congress Cataloging-in-Publication Data
Dill-Shackleford, Karen, 1969–
Mad men unzipped : fans on sex, love, and the sixties on TV /
by Karen Dill-Shackleford, Cynthia Vinney, Jerri Lynn Hogg, and
Kristin Hopper-Losenicky.
pages   cm
Includes bibliographical references and index.
ISBN 978-1-60938-377-0 (pbk), ISBN 978-1-60938-378-7 (ebk)
1. Mad men (Television program) 2. Nineteen sixties. 3. Television
programs — Social aspects — United States. I. Vinney, Cynthia, 1978–
II. Hogg, Jerri Lynn. III. Hopper-Losenicky, Kristin, 1984– IV. Title.
PN1992.77.M226D55   2015
791.45′72 — dc23   2015008646

For the fans, present and future

Contents

Acknowledgments

Thank you to the cast and crew of *Mad Men*, as well as to the show's wonderful fans.

Thanks also to Don Grant, Lisa Swain, and Lynne Webb for ideas and support.

Thank you to Juan-Carlos Duran, Kelley Micuda, and Patrick McNabb for data processing and coding.

A great big thank you to Catherine Cocks, our editor at the University of Iowa Press. This book wouldn't have happened without your interest and invitation. You challenged us and made our writing better. We are grateful.

The encouragement, support, and patience of our families throughout this process has been invaluable. We couldn't have done it without them.

Thank you all for the inspiration behind this book.

Mad Men Unzipped

CHAPTER ONE

The *Mad Men* Fan Phenomenon

When *Mad Men* hit the airwaves in the fall of 2007, the bold, brash out-rageousness of the show started a buzz. Who were these chain-smoking, three-martini-lunching hipsters from a bygone era? More importantly, what could they tell us about ourselves? *Mad Men*, a show about Madison Avenue advertising executives of the 1960s, may have looked old school to some, but it had a freshness and an audacity that told the world it was a new kind of show. Soon we found that not only was *Mad Men* a refreshing novelty, but its flavor attracted the discerning fan, hungry for the kind of substance this at once swanky and thought-provoking venue would provide in spades.

This is the story of the *Mad Men* fan phenomenon: how the show and its fans distinguished themselves in a market where it's hard to make an impres-sion, not unlike the driven ad execs at the center of the story. As psychologists as well as members of the *Mad Men* audience, we've followed the show and the fans' reactions to better understand both fandom generally and the *Mad Men* fan phenomenon particularly.

This book represents cutting-edge psychological research on how fans make meaning from fictional drama. Using online fan commentary, we piece together some of the thought-provoking real-life issues that *Mad Men* fans use the show to better understand. On another level, we explore the chang-ing face of fandom and how *Mad Men* fans represent a kind of fan not rep-resented by the misguided stereotype of the geeky fan who has had a mental break with reality. In fact, we explain how being a fan of compelling story makes one *more* discerning about reality. More on that in chapter 2.

But first, a spoiler alert: because this book is designed primarily for fans who know these stories well, our chapters will be replete with spoilers. If you haven't watched more than a few episodes of *Mad Men*, put this book down, fire up your Netflix account, and catch up before reading on.

The Plot

It has been said that *Mad Men* is a show about the American dream — whether it be won, lost, or otherwise. It is, of course, a period piece, the titular phrase referring to the men of Madison Avenue in New York City who worked in the ad game in the 1960s. This setting allowed the show's creators to shine a light on a number of issues, most notably the sexual politics and the working world of that era. Some view the show as the story of one American family, led by unlikely patriarch Don Draper, himself raised in a brothel, largely by stepparents and incidental players in his life. In that view, Don and his wife Betty represent an ideal, albeit a complicated one, of what a man and woman are supposed to be — beautiful, successful parents with money and all the finer things. On the inside there are deep cracks that surface readily, revealing what's wrong with the culture at the same time it reveals our own humanity as we struggle with identity.

Another perspective on the show is that it is about Don and Peggy, a man and a woman scratching and clawing to stay alive in the cutthroat world of advertising on Madison Avenue in the 1960s. Peggy considers Don her mentor, and she may well be his mirror. Through Don's and Peggy's missteps and forward lurches, we see how it was for a man and for a woman to pursue the American dream of high-stakes business in that era.

Scholars say that one of the reasons we love period pieces in fiction is that they allow us to feel a sort of superiority at how evolved we've become since those bygone days when folks had it much worse than we do now. It doesn't matter if we're talking about *Masters of Sex*, *Downton Abbey*, or *Mad Men* ... they each offer an opportunity to appreciate the progress that has been made since that time in history.

Perhaps that vantage point was the first thing audiences noticed about *Mad Men*. We remember the buzz surrounding the early days of the show, when friends asked each other, "Have you seen that new show, *Mad Men*?" This question was usually followed by wide-eyed descriptions of women's place in the work world of the 1960s, how much people smoked and drank back then, or the way men in the office unapologetically hit on the "girls."

For those of us who were not old enough to remember those days, we felt that we were witnessing them firsthand through the eyes of our favorite char-acters. For those of us who were there, it sparked memories from our lives at that time. And as the series moved through its 1960s timeline, we lived through history with the characters. We watched them react to the Kennedy and King assassinations and to Ali knocking out Liston. We were voyeurs as they watched the moon landing and followed the Cuban missile crisis, all from our modern vantage point, where we know how these stories end. We saw their reactions and their lives played out while history rolled by on their screens and over their airwaves.

Mad Men's Place in TV History

And speaking of history, *Mad Men* has its own unique place in television his-tory. Produced as original content for American cable channel AMC, it was the first such drama to win an Emmy. This made AMC the come-from-behind dark horse of original content that other channels and streaming sources wanted to emulate. The show has been critically acclaimed from the beginning and during its seven-season run has continued to garner accolades. It's been listed as one of the best television dramas of all time by the likes of *TV Guide*, *Rolling Stone*, IMDb, and the *New York Daily News*. In fact, it is consistently listed as one of the best television series of all time — period. For example, the prestigious *Writers' Guild of America* ranked it among the ten best-written TV series ever.

In late 2014, Google counted *Mad Men* among the ten most talked-about shows on the Internet, and the show is listed among the top television series to watch on Netflix. Meanwhile, IMDb reports that *Mad Men* has been nomi-nated for 247 major awards and has won eighty-five of them. This includes a whopping 105 Emmy nominations and fifteen Emmy wins: four for out-standing drama series, three for outstanding writing for a drama series, and one for outstanding main title design. *Mad Men* also earned three Golden Globe awards for best drama series. And the cast won two Screen Actors Guild Awards for outstanding performance by an ensemble in a drama series. These stats place *Mad Men* firmly in company with other dramatic fan favor-ites like *The Sopranos*, *Breaking Bad*, *Game of Thrones*, *Law and Order*, and *The West Wing*.

Figure 1. Peggy Olson Barbie doll. Photo by Michael Williams/MyLifeInPlastic.com.

There is even a set of *Mad Men* Barbie dolls, immortalizing four of the show's main characters: Don and Betty Draper, Roger Sterling, and Joan Harris/Holloway. We can only imagine the fun that fans have playing *Mad Men* Barbies. In fact, some of us are wishing for these toys in our Christmas stockings. Since they are limited edition dolls, this may be a pricey holiday treat. The Joan and Betty dolls have sold on Amazon for about $200 each!

Not lucky enough to have your own official *Mad Men* Barbies? If you are creative enough, you can make your own. Artist Michael Williams has lovingly and painstakingly styled a troop of Barbie and Ken dolls to resemble the characters on the show. We love this delightful tableau featuring own working girl, Peggy Olson, as an at-the-office action figure. Peggy has a set of accessories including her Heinz campaign and a "wad of cash from Roger."

Our Approach

We, your authors and tour guides through this journey into Madison Avenue of the 1960s, are a team of media psychologists. We study the interactions between people and media—from smart phones to Twitter, from film and television to iPods and Apple watches. Two areas of media psychology that are at center stage in this book are: 1) the way people make sense of fictional stories and use what they learn to think about life and 2) how the interactive world of social media allows us to contribute to the conversation. We will talk more about fan psychology and fans as story contributors in chapter 2. For now, we'll simply set the stage by saying that we'll present both voices in this book: the voice of the story itself and the voice of the fans who add their experiences and interpretations to the story.

The Figures at Center Stage in Our Story

Though the show is blooming with personalities and has quite an impressive array of supporting roles, at the core are six main players. These are Don Draper (born Dick Whitman), Betty Draper (later Francis), Peggy Olson, Roger Sterling, Joan Holloway (later Harris), and Pete Campbell. Supporting characters on the home front include Sally Draper (Don and Betty's daughter), Megan Draper (Don's—technically—third wife), Henry Francis (Betty's second husband), Mona Sterling and Jane Sterling (Roger's first and second wives), Margaret Sterling (Roger's daughter), Trudy Campbell (Pete's wife), Katherine Olson and Anita Olson (Peggy's mother and sister), Dr. Greg Harris (Joan's husband), and Gail Holloway (Joan's mother).

As mentioned earlier, the icon at the center of the *Mad Men* phenomenon is Don Draper: successful ad man, drinker, philanderer, and questionable parent. It is Don's image we see in the opening credits of the show. Don's silhouette falls from the sky past the ad-festooned buildings of Madison Avenue, selling sex, style, and savoir faire. How can a show that's largely about

Don Draper seemingly kill him off during the opening titles? We address the final story arc and series ending in the epilogue of this book.

In an interview with Stephen Colbert in 2014, show creator Matthew Weiner spoke about the inspiration for the Don Draper character. Weiner said that he saw Don as someone trying to live up to all the mixed messages from the show's era about what it means to be a man. To be a real man meant to sleep with a string of beautiful women, to drink and smoke, to be a cutthroat executive who also scored at the office, all the while being the head of a family and a good father and husband.

Actor Jon Hamm, who plays Draper, rose to fame in that role. Early in the show's run, Hamm hosted *Saturday Night Live* for the first time. In the opening monologue he quipped that the first thing people ask him is "What's *Mad Men*?" and the second thing is "What's AMC?" Hamm beat out eighty other actors who auditioned for the role of Don Draper.

Weiner felt there was a connection between Draper and Hamm because they both lost their parents when they were young. Young Don Draper (then Dick Whitman) never knew his mother, a prostitute, and his father died in front of him when he was ten. Jon Hamm's mother died when he was ten, and his father died when he was twenty. Both also faced struggles to advance in their careers. When Hamm auditioned for *Mad Men*, he was having trouble getting cast as an actor and hadn't gotten a single role during his first three years in LA. He'd made a deal with himself that if he reached thirty without career success, he would go back home to St. Louis. But after earning the part of Don Draper, his career took off. As we know, he hit the jackpot with *Mad Men*, as did Weiner and AMC.

In the world of *Mad Men*, as we get to know Don Draper, we gradually learn about his childhood as Dick Whitman. On the heels of his turbulent upbringing, he goes off to fight in Korea. Through a freak accident, the real Don Draper is killed, and the young man — Dick Whitman — assumes Don's name and is sent home. This is a secret that will unravel throughout the show as we play with the concept of identity and hidden secrets. Later, Dick (now Don) learns that the real Don Draper's wife, Anna Draper, is still alive. He meets her, and they become very close. In many ways Anna and her niece Stephanie are Don's real family. This family relationship spawns two of our favorite *Mad Men* quotes about identity and self-knowledge: In season four, episode three, Stephanie says to Don, "Nobody knows what's wrong with themselves, and everyone else can see it right away." In season four, episode eight, Don says, "People tell you who they are, but we ignore it — because we want them to be who we want them to be."

On the Home Front

Meanwhile, in the world of *Mad Men*, hanging out on the home front in Ossining, New York, is Don's wife, Betty. Betty, like Don, is a controversial character who elicits both scorn and affection from the fans. Since Betty's role relates to women's roles, we'll focus attention on her in the chapters where we address the fans' impressions of topics such as parenting and gender roles in *Mad Men*. After the demise of Don's relationship with Betty, he marries Megan, an aspiring actress who eventually discovers her autonomy from Don after making a real go of a relationship with him. Megan's is a more complex role and her character, like Peggy's, represents the evolution of women in the sixties. Megan moves from secretary to ad woman to New York actress to Hollywood bohemian and career woman, eventually growing past Don.

Given Don's seeming addiction to women, there are also a host of mistresses and one-night stands. In fact, there are a number of fan- and professionally generated lists of Don's conquests available online. For instance, the Daily Beast promises an accounting of "every woman Don Draper has hooked up with." Notables on the list include Midge Daniels (the bohemian artist), Rachel Menken (the Jewish business heiress), Bobbie Barrett (the comedian's wife), Joy (the California girl who picked Don out of a crowd), Suzanne Farrell (the schoolteacher), Allison (the naive secretary), Dr. Faye Miller (the advertising psychologist), Sylvia Rosen (his neighbor in the apartment building where he lives with Megan), and of course, Megan (originally his secretary) and Betty (a Bryn Mawr graduate whom he met while she was a New York model). Nerve.com ranks Don's top relationships, from most to least dysfunctional, as follows: 9) Allison, 8) Bobbie, 7) Betty, 6) Suzanne, 5) Joy, 4) Megan, 3) Midge, 2) Rachel, and 1) Dr. Faye.

Blogger Sonia Saraiya confesses:

I'm both besotted with and disgusted by Don Draper, who somehow manages to be both tenderly flawed and nakedly brutal at the same time. Don burns through women faster than some people change socks. Some of those women try to change him (and fail). Some try to redeem him (and fail). Some try to find some spark of humanity in him to connect with (and fail disastrously). Many have amazing sex with him, but so far, none have saved him.

At the Office

At Don's side beginning with the pilot episode is Peggy Olson, young, naive, and surprisingly ambitious, given the era she grew up in. Peggy starts work as Don's secretary and then rises to join the creative team at Sterling Cooper ad agency, where she eventually becomes a leader. Since Peggy's role is associated with the working world, we'll focus more on her and how the fans see her when we talk about gender and office politics later on. Elisabeth Moss, who plays Peggy, was also a recurring character on another critically acclaimed drama, *The West Wing*. In an interview Matthew Weiner confesses that Peggy is the character who most reminds him of himself. And many in the audience identify with Peggy early on as she struggles to find her place while showing that she has a good heart and good intentions.

Also in the heat of the game at the office are three additional lead characters: Joan Harris/Holloway, Roger Sterling, and Pete Campbell. A fan favorite from the beginning, we follow Joan's life as the aspiring head of the secretarial pool and sleeping with Roger Sterling to her wild ride with client Jaguar that leads to her unlikely addition to the partners' team.

At home Joan looks for a husband, finds one and leaves him, and ends up raising a son (who is actually Roger's) with her mother by her side. One of our favorite moments with Joan is when, after exercising saint-like patience with husband Greg, she is asked by him whether she knows what it's like to want something all her life, to work for it, and never get it. Her spot-on response: to smash a sizeable vase on his head. You will hear more later about Joan and how the fans followed her life at home and at work.

Back at the office, Roger Sterling is certainly a trip. (At times he's literally tripping, right? Rim shot!) Some say *Mad Men* is about seeking true happiness and false happiness, the difference between the surface and the soul, between swimming in the shallows and diving deeply into life. Roger takes us places both shallow and deep. In a deeper moment we see him holding hands with wife Jane during an LSD trip, coming to terms with their true feelings for each other. On the surface is the debonair silver fox, tossing out one-liners from a seemingly endless storehouse of quips. In fact, Vulture.com hosts a blog called the "Complete Quips of Roger Sterling." Some of our favorite lines that hint at Roger's personal philosophy of life are set out in table 1.

In the aforementioned Stephen Colbert interview, Matthew Weiner said that ad executive Pete Campbell was the man Weiner wanted to be when he was in high school. Pete is the consummate hungry businessman who'll sell his (perhaps nonexistent) soul for a well-heeled client. Pete is hard to love sometimes, like when he forces himself on the au pair girl next door the weekend his wife leaves town, or when he cringes as he sees Peggy with a baby (since Peggy secretly had Pete's baby and gave it up).

GQ described Pete Campbell as "the petulant, permanently dissatisfied coworker." Meanwhile, Pete's idea of a compliment is calling Peggy — the person who may know him best in the world — "every bit as good as any woman in this business." But what can we say about Pete Campbell that's not encapsulated by the Internet sensation the character spawned: Pete Campbell's Bitchface? Pete Campbell's Bitchface is an example of an Internet meme or a piece of media, such as a video or image, that goes viral.

Memes can center on a single video or a style of images such as LOL cats, which feature pictures of cat antics accompanied by messages in LOLspeak, which is a style of writing (for more on this, visit icanhas.cheezburger.com and knowyourmeme.com). The Pete Campbell's Bitchface meme has a dedicated Tumblr site, describing itself as "a tumblog" (read: tumblr blog) dedicated to everyone's favorite "little shit" from *Mad Men* and his endlessly glorious facial expressions. We'll share one here (figure 2). You can also check it out at http://petecampbellsbitchface.tumblr.com/.

Enlivening the office is a troop of intriguing supporting characters. These include a shifting team of partners such as Bert Cooper (eccentric cofounder

"Reservations at home. I've had those. Easiest ones to break." (s1, e7)

"At some point, we've all parked in the wrong garage." (s1, e7)

"Can I just fire everyone?" (s2, e2)

"I'll bet she suffers in silence out there, hoping you'll notice her. Wait until she finds out about your Cadillac. She'll be waiting naked right in front of this window." (s2, e7)

(*On pregnant Betty*) "Oh, look. Princess Grace just swallowed a basketball." (s3, e2)

"Let me put it in account terms: Are you aware of the number of hand jobs I'm going to have to give?" (s3, e5)

"Have a drink. It'll make me look younger." (s4, e5)

(*On Ida Blankenship*) "She died like she lived: surrounded by the people she answered phones for." (s4, e9)

"As a wise man once said, the only thing worse than not getting what you want is someone else getting it." (s5, e1)

"Are you gonna tell me what you're going to talk about, or is my look of surprise part of the sales pitch?" (s5, e12)

"Well you know what they say about Detroit: it's all fun and games till they shoot you in the face." (s6, e13)

(*On his mother's funeral*) "I looked out on that crowd, and all I saw was a bunch more women I disappointed." (s6, e1)

(*On Don vomiting*) "He was just saying what everybody else was thinking." (s6, e2)

"We're getting a computer. It's gonna do lots of magical things, like make Harry Crane seem important." (s7, e4)

Table 1. Selected gems from "The Complete Quips of Roger Sterling" by Gwynne Watkins at Vulture.com. (Access the entire list at http://www.vulture.com/2013/04 /mad-men-complete-quips-of-roger-sterling.html.)

Figure 2. An image from the "Pete Campbell's Bitchface" meme.

of Sterling Cooper), Lane Pryce (head of the British invasion), Ted Chaough (Peggy's erstwhile lover and Don's erstwhile rival in the ad game), and Jim Cutler (originally one of Ted's partners, then a partner at the re-formed Sterling Cooper & Partners).

As the company changes from Sterling Cooper to Sterling Cooper Draper Pryce to Sterling Cooper & Partners, notable team members include Ken Cosgrove (reluctant favorite of the Chevy guys, reluctant rival to Pete Campbell), Harry Crane (who knows TV is the next big thing), Paul Kinsey (part copywriter, part Bohemian wannabe), Freddy Rumsen (perhaps the truest vision of a struggling, then recovering, alcoholic), Stan Rizzo (creative who misses the old Peggy), Duck Phillips (fallen ad exec who also misses Peggy), and Michael Ginsberg (idealistic creative who ends up missing a nipple).

Best of the Best

We all have our favorite episodes of *Mad Men*, but some have received more attention than others. Three episodes have won Emmys for outstanding writing for a drama series. The first of these is the pilot, entitled "Smoke Gets in

Your Eyes." The second is season two's "Meditations in an Emergency," in which Betty discovers she is pregnant with baby Gene. The third is the season three finale, "Shut the Door. Have a Seat," in which big changes happen in the ad world and key players shift.

Rolling Stone and IMDb each published lists of their favorite *Mad Men* episodes, and both chose the same favorite: season four's "The Suitcase." "The Suitcase" finds Peggy and Don working late together at the office, despite the fact that it's Peggy's birthday and her boyfriend and family are trying to hold a surprise party in her honor at a Manhattan restaurant. Don wants to hold Peggy there to work on the Samsonite campaign. Eventually, Peggy makes the choice not only to stand up her boyfriend and family but to dump her boyfriend in favor of work because, as she says, nothing in the world outside the office seems as important as what's going on inside it.

"The Suitcase" is perhaps most notable because we see rare glimpses into certain facets of Peggy and Don and their relationship. We see both Don's sense of humor and also his vulnerability (in dealing with the passing of his dear friend Anna). We see Peggy's frustration at what she believes is Don's lack of gratitude for her work and a bit of her feelings about giving up her baby. Maybe most importantly for fans, we see what Don and Peggy's relationship is made of.

Fandom, *Mad Men* Style

Just as *Mad Men* is known for its attractive style, its fans came on the scene sporting their own stylish signature as well. Of course, *Mad Men* fans are enthusiastic. Vulture.com ranked *Mad Men* as being in the top twenty-five fandoms of all times, alongside perennial fan favorites like *Star Trek*, *Doctor Who*, and *Harry Potter*.

Mad Men fans tend to be more affluent than other fan bases. About half the *Mad Men* audience make more than $100,000 per year. They are likely to be following other complex, critically acclaimed dramas such as *The Sopranos*. They are perhaps less about cosplay (fans dressing in costumes depicting their favorite characters) and cons (fan conventions) than they are about deep exploration of themes, story, character, and craft (though it should be noted that *Mad Men* fans enjoy their own sort of cosplay that is more likely to take place at a party than at a con). Basically, *Mad Men* fans practice their own brand of art appreciation and literary criticism, their text and tableaux being visual media. One might say that if *Mad Men* fans were a beverage, they would be a fine wine decanted for a discerning palette.

The very book you are holding is a testament to the deliberations and insights of *Mad Men* fans. In the chapters that follow, the fans will speak in their own words. We'll learn how they make sense of everything from Betty's parenting to Roger's drinking, from Peggy's pregnancy to Joan's decision to sleep with the client from Jaguar. This is what *Mad Men* fans do—they watch episodes carefully. Devotees look for opportunities for meaning making. Committed viewers deconstruct like literary scholars, thinking about story arcs like screenwriters, and deriving meaning from the experience.

Lovers of all things *Mad Men* can be found everywhere—many sites are devoted to blogging and commenting about *Mad Men*. Two of the most loved fan sites are the essential "Basket of Kisses" (recalling Peggy's entrée into the world of ad copy) at lippsisters.com and "Footnotes of Mad Men" at madmenunbuttoned.com. These and many other sites find viewers recapping new story lines, talking history, gender, and politics, and exclaiming over the latest plot shock or behind-the-scenes story.

Fans as Fashionistas, Artists, and Storytellers

Of course, like Roger Sterling, *Mad Men* fans also know how to have fun and how to do it with style. Since we don't live in the world of the 1960s, where room-sized computers frighten the nipples off us, we need only visit the Internet to see what fans are inventing, sharing, and experiencing.

Mad Men and style go together like Joan Harris and Harris tweed. *Mad Men* inspired an entire line of clothing at Banana Republic and a suit at Brooks Brothers. And if *Mad Men* fans aren't as keen on big conventions like Comicon, they are definitely into the swankier and more exclusive venues and fetes. Maybe they aren't to be found camping out at Comicon and eating overpriced fair food, but they are prone to throwing private *Mad Men*–inspired parties. There are also *Mad Men* weekends at wineries and other

Figure 3. Cosplay at our university offices — staff member dresses as Betty Draper. (Thank you, Sophia at Fielding Graduate University.)

high-brow affairs. Likewise there are *Mad Men*–inspired fashion blogs, books, and cookbooks. Like Joan Harris and Roger Sterling, *Mad Men* fans are likely to think a good party involves champagne, mid-century gowns, and a romantic session on the office sofa. Riding mowers are, of course, now discouraged at such fetes.

In the cosplay department, rather than showing up at a big con, they may prefer getting their Don Draper on at an office or house party. For example, here is a fan (our real life colleague Sophia) dressed as Betty Draper (figure 3).

Fans also write stories about their favorite characters in a genre known as "fan fiction." What is fan fiction (aka "fan fic"), and why do fans produce it?

Fan fiction is written by fans and takes place in the universe of the favorite story. Fans produce fan fic so they can explore the story lines they love further. Some fans create fan fiction because they want to add to or alter the content of the story world. For example, fans may wish that two characters who are not together on *Mad Men*, like Peggy and Don, would get together. So they write a fan fic story in which Peggy and Don have a romantic relationship. Or perhaps a *Mad Men* fan is disappointed in Don's flawed parenting, so they write a story in which Don treats Sally with the love and respect these fans feel Sally is due. In this way fan fiction can be a kind of wish fulfillment exercise.

In our digital era stories live in what are known as "transmedia spaces." Transmedia means that the story crosses from one medium to another (TV, blog, fan video, theater, app), playing itself out in different spaces. We want the world of *Mad Men* to live on, not only as streaming video on our television or computer screens, but as textual fan-fiction stories on the web, beautiful Emmy ads festooned on highway billboards, and tweets peppering our smartphones with pithy content.

As long as we're reminiscing about fandom and about all the firsts associated with *Mad Men*, we have to talk about the *Mad Men* Twitter intrigue. First, short-form fan fic was, in and of itself, a novelty. Furthermore, the intrigue to which we allude also had legs as a kind of the-fan-versus-"the man" clash.

What happened was that a few *Mad Men* fans grabbed Twitter accounts under the names of their favorite characters (such as @BettyDraper) and started tweeting as if they were those characters. By all accounts each of them put a great deal of energy and care into their tweets. Some said that the amount of research that went into making the tweets authentic was almost like having a second job.

Then something newsworthy happened—the fans' accounts were suspended after Twitter misunderstood an inquiry from AMC about the identities behind the accounts and responded to it as a takedown request. This prompted an outcry from fans to which AMC responded by allowing the fans' accounts to be reinstated. The consensus from fans and onlookers alike was "you can't buy this kind of good press" and "why look a gift horse in the mouth?" Indeed, Helen Klein Ross, who tweeted as Betty Draper, actually works in advertising, as did other *Mad Men* Twitterers. She thought that it would be great fun to get Betty's tweets throughout the day, as if we were connected by these messages to Betty's everyday life off camera.

In one experiment, a group of fans tweeting as show characters filled in scenes that were not included on the show by "live" tweeting the Beatles concert at Shea Stadium with which Don surprised Sally in the episode "Hands and Knees" (season four, episode ten). The fans called what they produced a "twepisode." During the twepisode, @DonDraperSCDP tweeted, "Hat? Check. Coat? Check. Smokes? Check. Tickets?" and "Don't worry @Sally_Draper, we won't miss the Beatles." Then Helen Klein Ross grabbed some of these tweets and wove them into a video story, which she posted. This is a great example of transmedia fan fic that went viral. We won't say much more, for now, about fan fic of either the long or short variety because we devote a whole chapter to the subject.

And fans don't restrict themselves to mere words. Perhaps it's no surprise that *Mad Men*'s famous style is reflected in the quality of the art that fans produce. For instance, one piece of fan art depicts a scene from an episode entitled "The Beautiful Girls" (season four, episode nine), where Roger selects a pair of twins for a "private audition" in the executive offices. (Go to our companion web site to see it.) This rendezvous ends badly, with Roger suffering a heart attack. Before leaving for the hospital, he quips, "Dammit, I don't want to die in this office. . . . If it looks like I'm going, open a window. I'd rather flatten the top of a cab" (S4, E9).

Later in the book we discuss sexism and the role of women in *Mad Men*. This fan art, and the episode that inspired it, raises the issue of how fans react to touchstone moments involving sexism and characters using and abusing each other. For now, we concentrate on the art itself, pausing to say that the art generated by fans shares much in common with the fan comments we present here — they represent fan reactions to the moments that stood out for them and a desire to share their interpretations with others.

Speaking of iconic images that might offend, another fan makes a joke by combining two pop-culture memes — a skit from *Saturday Night Live* called "Dick in a Box" and the iconic image of Don Draper, whose real name is

Dick. (Go to our companion web site to see it.) This, of course, sends the message that the real Don is a real Dick. Or, as one of the fans who provided material for our research dubbed him, "Don Dick Cheating I-Have-No-People Whitman Draper Lying Liarface." We couldn't have said it better ourselves. Another clever fan art piece combines a well-known object with the many shades and moods of *Mad Men*. Created by artist Emily Miethner, it is called *The Periodic Table of Mad Men*. The table includes favorite themes like harsh '60s realities, cultural references, intoxicants, and disappointments. (Go to our companion web site to see it.)

Finally, also combining art with pithy commentary, we have the "Mad Men Chart of Goodness." (Go to our companion web site to see it.) This chart features nine key characters laid out in a grid, *Brady Bunch* style. On one side is a continuum from good through neutral to evil. On the other side is philosophical style, from lawful through neutral to chaotic. For example, we have Roger Sterling landing in the neutral evil box. Alongside him is a representative quote, "What I'm saying is I want what I want." Opposite Roger, on the side of good, is Peggy, representing "neutral good" by saying, "I don't think anybody wants to be one of a hundred colors in a box."

Such art is not only fun and attractive, but it is a representation of the kind of ongoing discussion that fans can have with each other in the era of modern social media. Such images go viral and spark discussion. One fan might argue with another fan's characterization of someone as good, evil, or neutral. One fan might say that Joan is, in fact, more "good" than Peggy or that Don cannot be considered "neutral." Still others may disagree, and the debate continues. Along the way we learn some things about life and about ourselves.

Some of the memes that fans have created have gone viral—like the one known affectionately as Pete Campbell's Bitchface. Another source of great fun among fans is the Sad Don Draper meme. Sad Don Draper followed the Sad Keanu meme, which featured an image of the actor Keanu Reeves looking sad with various humorous captions and in various humorous contexts. *Mad Men* fans stirred up their own hilarity with images of Don Draper crying superimposed in contexts such as famous sad scenes or things that would make Don cry. The crying image was taken from the aforementioned episode "The Suitcase," in which Don breaks down after the loss of Anna Draper.

Fans photobombed this crying Don into other emotional scenes, such as the double-rainbow meme or the hospital scene from the movie *Up*. One of our favorites is a Sad Don Draper crying upon seeing an airplane's "no smoking" sign. There are, of course, Sad Don Draper Facebook and Tumblr pages. If you want to follow this meme, or others like it, check out knowyourmeme .com for more info. Sad Don Draper stats can be found at http://knowyour meme.com/memes/sad-don-draper.

We know that *Mad Men* is known for its visual art and style, including its Emmy Award–winning opening titles. The image of Don Draper, seated with his arm draped over the back of a sofa, cigarette in hand, is iconic. Fans have altered that image in many swanky and humorous ways. This visual meme is known as "Draping," named, of course, for the draping action of the arm and for our hero, Don Draper. A Draping Tumblr page was launched, as were Facebook and Pinterest pages. And fans tweet their own shots of themselves, their pets, kids, or even objects draping, marked, of course, by #draping. Read more at http://knowyourmeme.com/memes/draping.

Betty Draper gets plenty of attention, too. *New York* magazine created a *Mad Men*–inspired viral video that is a montage called "Ugly Betty," featuring "classic" Betty Draper mothering moments. It includes scenes in which Betty throws out such parenting gems as "Go watch TV," "Go bang your head against a wall," and the ever-popular "Sally looks fat." *Parenting* magazine columnist Kate Goodin commented that watching the video brought to mind the old days, when parents were not driving their kids to soccer practice or paying as much attention to them in general. She cites Betty's parenting as an example, saying that Betty's only advice for activities involves either going upstairs or watching TV. Goodin also notes that watching Betty in action may make us all feel like better parents. Watch the video and see if you agree: http://www.vulture.com/2010/07/mad_mens_betty_drapers_guide_t.html.

There is also an endless supply of stills from *Mad Men* that fans caption. One site that hosts these images is the "Mean *Mad Men*" site on Tumblr: http://meanmadmen.tumblr.com/. Another is "*Mad Men* Logic" at http:// www.quickmeme.com/Madmen-Logic/page/4/. On this page fans can add to a picture of Don Draper smoking a caption such as "Just finished a ciga-

Figure 4. Betty's got a gun. Betty, ever the practical gal,
takes care of business in the back yard. (Scene from season 1,
episode 9, "Shoot.")

rette. Perfect time for a cigarette." Another funny site is called "Mad Men
Screenshots with Things Drawn on Them." The site features, as expected,
Mad Men screenshots with things drawn on them (at http://madmenwith
thingsdrawnonthem.tumblr.com/page/3). For example, take a shot of Peggy
giving a presentation, which has been labeled, "Essentially, I am amazing,"
and a shot of an admiring Don looking on, saying, "Heck, yeah, you are Pegs."

AMC joined in on some of the viral fun by creating the "*Mad Men* Yourself" app. In the app you can customize your avatar, complete with *Mad Men*
accessories, such as stylish clothes, cigarettes, and booze, and story line–
relevant accessories such as a rifle (perhaps from Betty's adventures with the
neighbor's pet birds—see figure 4—or from Pete's office shenanigans with
another rifle).

As the final mini-season approached, AMC announced a contest called
"*Mad Men*: The Fan Cut." AMC invited fans to act out the first episode,
"Smoke Gets in Your Eyes," scene by scene and to submit their offering online. Rob Dean, blogger for the AV Club, quipped that this invitation was
an excellent opportunity to use that Vincent Kartheiser (aka Pete Campbell)
impression you've been working on. This fan-cut idea is a notable good step
in AMC's cultivation and appreciation of its fans.

Now that we've talked a bit about *Mad Men* as fan phenomenon, we next turn our attention toward some psychological and media theories that help us better explain the fan experience. We also talk more about how we conducted our original psychological research on *Mad Men* fans as they dissect this thought-provoking and entertaining story.

CHAPTER TWO

How Their Lives Touched Ours

Do you remember a scene from *Mad Men* that made you cry or cheer? Did Don, Betty, or Pete ever make you so angry that you found yourself brooding about it days after the show aired? Did watching Peggy's or Joan's struggles and triumphs ever make you feel like you were right there with her, feeling what she was feeling?

If you are like us, the answer to all of those questions is a resounding yes. Whatever characters you love or love to hate (and, we know, sometimes it changes week by week), they can really get under your skin. We have spent hours talking together about *Mad Men*. We have shared stories about being moved to tears when Don brought his kids to see the brothel where he was raised. We have talked about feeling protective of Sally. At least one of us frequently wants to punch Pete Campbell right in the Bitchface (thank you, Lane, for helping her live the dream — and see figure 19 to relive it now with us).

We all have our lists of *Mad Men* scenes that are burned into our brains. For example, we can't forget the car ride where Don brought Sally back to school and she left him with the words, "Happy Valentine's Day. I love you." We get irritated thinking about Pete's famous declaration about Peggy being as good as any woman at her job. Like many fans, we think about the times when dance scenes moved us. For example, the touching segments when Don and Peggy danced together in "The Suitcase" (figure 5) and "The Strategy." Or when Peggy did the twist for (the twisted?) Pete Campbell.

Of course, Megan doing the sexy dance and singing "Zou Bisou Bisou" for Don on his fortieth birthday will go down as one of the most remembered *Mad Men* moments. *Entertainment Weekly* called the embrace on "The Strategy" "the TV moment that launched a thousand tweets." *Time Magazine* said that the buzz around "Zou Bisou Bisou" was a producer's dream,

Figure 5. Some say that Peggy is Don's mirror. One of the few women Don hasn't slept with, Don sometimes pushes Peggy hard to excel. In that context, this tender moment between the two, mixing work and affection, really resonated with fans.

while *USA Today* chimed in that "Jessica Paré gets the world humming Zou Bisou Bisou."

In addition to watching the show ourselves, we have another perspective—one that comes from analyzing large collections of fan comments from the perspective of media psychologists. Many times, while reading their thoughts, we knew exactly how fans felt—we've felt like that ourselves. Other times fans surprised us with their views, whether venomous, loving, insightful, or sometimes all of the above. In both cases we learned something about how media work on our emotions and how we use the media to understand ourselves.

Mad Men Through the Fans' Eyes

For over a year our research team has been tracking and analyzing the social media comments of *Mad Men* fans. This team effort involves some pretty intense searching, organizing, and cataloging of what we found in order to distill and analyze the meaning of what the fans say about the show. We will describe this process further.

Throughout the book we move back and forth between conveying what

Figure 6. Megan Draper singing "Zou Bisou Bisou."

fans think and feel about *Mad Men* and how we understand both the show and the fans from our perspective as a team of media psychologists. We present research that communicates the thoughts of many fan voices. Then we situate this in the context of our theoretical understanding of the human attachment to characters and stories. Our emphasis is always on moving toward a better understanding of the role of story in our lives and on digging into the richness of that experience.

Methods to Our Madness

Social scientists describe their research procedures as "methods." This isn't a research textbook, so we'll keep this methods discussion to the broad strokes. For those of you not into science, we'll consider most of our methodology outside of your "need to know." For those of you who crush on science, we'll give you the basics here and refer you to the scientific journals for all the gory details.

We started our research with one major idea: we wanted to discover what fans think and feel about their experiences with *Mad Men*. If you don't live in the world of psychology research, we can tell you that in many ways social media are a research psychologist's wildest dreams come true. This is because today people share their thoughts and feelings publicly on the Internet so they are ripe for picking by the over-excited mad (men?!) scientist. We don't have to find *Mad Men* fans and drag them into the lab—their views are already online to be read and considered.

Scientists are organized, if nothing else. So we organized a series of steps to systematically gather online fan comments. We started with a particular topic, such as parenting on *Mad Men*. We ran key words through search engines, including Google and Bing, and generated a list of blog comments that discussed our topic and contained fan comments on those blog posts. Next, we collected the fan comments, making sure that the ones we included in our analyses were on topic. Note that this means we harvested by topic at the comment level rather than at the blog level. We kept these blog comments anonymous by removing all user names and other identifying information—this is both for ethical reasons (privacy and protection of individuals) and also for practical reasons—most of the comments do not give the commenter's name or gender. And if they did, we wouldn't have a way of verifying their authenticity. So, in our discussion of the fan voice, remember that these comments are anonymous and that we do not know demographics such as the gender, age, or race of the commenters.

Next came two different trajectories—one in which the data were organized automatically by the computer and another in which human beings organized the data according to a prearranged set of criteria. We refer to the former as the "big data" approach and the latter as the "expert" approach.

For the big data approach we ran all the comments through a software program made to process large amounts of text for meaning. In mere minutes this software can tell us the major themes present in a large amount of data. This software is smart. It adjusts for English language usage, takes out superfluous words (so the word "the" isn't always the top theme), and determines how the emerging themes are interconnected. It also draws word clouds that represent the most prevalent themes and the interrelationships between concepts.

From there, for the expert approach, we put the data—or as much of it as humans can reasonably code in several hours—into a different software program that allows researchers to mark fan comments, categorizing them by topic. Think of it as sorting comments into different baskets by theme. One comment can go in a number of baskets if it represents more than one theme.

Together these two approaches give us, as scientists, two viewpoints on the same fan insights, one whose strengths include objectivity, speed, and volume, and the other whose strengths include expert human judgment and the systematic smart application of knowledge. All of this careful processing, whether by human or machine, is designed with one purpose — to summarize for you what *Mad Men* fans think about the show, its characters, situations, and meanings.

For example, in response to a blog entitled "Mad Men Is a Cautionary Tale about Alcoholism," one commenter wrote, "*Mad Men* is a cautionary tale about a lot of things, alcoholism being one of them, but aside from its most visible example of alcoholism, *Mad Men* is an exploration of defining meaning as a human being and ways of expressing ourselves in a profound way."

Is *Mad Men* a cautionary tale? Some fans do interpret the show this way, whether the cautionary tale is about alcohol, cigarettes, shallow consumerism, or unbridled avarice. Some say that *Mad Men* is, more specifically, a cautionary tale about gender roles. In fact, when new fans first began to buzz about the show, it was the outmoded gender politics that captured the imagination of many fans. Because of this emphasis on the show, we devote quite a bit of time and space to unpacking how the fans digest the way *Mad Men* addresses gender politics.

We have individual chapters on the exploration of men and of women in the *Mad Men* universe. We address office politics through the lens of gender and the unique perspectives of different characters. Another gender-related topic is parenthood. We see how fans understand key characters and story lines viewing the characters as parents, partners, and people.

Mad Men is a drama about life in the advertising world of the 1960s on Madison Avenue. Thus, one of our chapters addresses this world of advertising: its themes, mores, and deeper meaning. In this chapter we use additional research methods — we survey Mad Men fans who work in the advertising industry today, and we even interview a real-life former Mad Man who worked on Madison Avenue during the 1960s. These techniques enable us to investigate the perspectives of a specific group of fans whose ties to advertising cause them to feel personally connected to the show in special ways.

We also explore the *Mad Men* fans' perspective through the fan fiction they write and read. To study *Mad Men* fan fiction we used our big-data approach to analyze a large set of fan-written stories set in the *Mad Men* universe and featuring *Mad Men* characters. This allowed us to learn which characters and themes fan writers focus on the most. We also surveyed *Mad Men* fan-fiction writers and readers so they could describe in their own words what the show and fan fiction based on it means to them. Fan fiction, as you'll see, enables us to understand how fans make sense of the story and characters, what story lines they wish to explore further, and the things they wish they could change about the show.

And who could talk about *Mad Men* without mentioning sex? From Don's serial philandering, to the exploration of homosexuality, to women's sexuality in the sixties, there is a lot of ground to cover here. In fact, we had originally wanted to include a chapter on addiction as well—including alcohol and sex addiction. Turns out that the fans had precious little to say about alcohol addiction that went beyond "that's how it was in those days." What they did want to talk about was sex addiction. So there will be plenty of sex talk later on.

Finally, what we saw over and over in our journey inside the fan mind was the importance of *Mad Men* as a period piece. This is reported in detail in the next chapter. Fans spent a great deal of time parsing the degree to which the personalities and events in *Mad Men* are timeless, as opposed to being mostly a reflection of a limited—and now bygone—period in history.

Cultural studies scholar Lynn Spigel says that we get a real sense of satisfaction when we view period television. According to her there are two kinds of history: history that comes from experts and history that comes from pop culture, such as television. Spigel claims that viewers construct their "popular memory" by viewing period pieces on television. She writes, "As I use the term, popular memory is history for the present; it is a mode of historical consciousness that speaks to the concerns and needs of contemporary life. Popular memory is a form of storytelling through which people make sense of their own lives and culture." Perhaps surprisingly, neither the history learned from textbooks nor the history learned from popular culture is entirely accurate. So we are left to think about what the truth really is. And the fans we studied did this quite a bit.

Just as our fans made sense of their lives by grappling with *Mad Men*, Spigel found that the college women she taught got many of their ideas about women in past eras from classic television. Although these women knew they "shouldn't" do this, they did it anyway, carving out beliefs, for example, about the typical 1950s housewife from shows like *Happy Days* (which, ironically, was also a period piece when it aired in the seventies). The research we relate here, and our own experience as fans, confirms that this is a very human approach to life — constructing fact from fiction.

Spigel says that we co-create a shared vision of history through popular culture. We can somehow simultaneously choose vintage shows to make fun of outmoded social roles and, at the same time, visit them for the pleasurable state of nostalgia they impart. In Spigel's words, "television engages in a kind of historical consciousness that remembers the past in order to believe in the progress of the present." We would add, based on our data, that watching *Mad Men* helps fans put not only their own memories in context but also the stories they have been told by friends and relatives about the past.

Fan Psychology

We believe that the research we performed enables us to better understand the ways we can wrestle with the big questions of life, understand issues and personalities, and connect to others struggling with the same questions through our fandom. Everyone is a fan of something. Most of us are experts on television, having grown up with it as a regular part of our lives. As media psychologists we try to understand more deeply the psychological processes underlying fandom.

One of the first things to understand is the importance of stories. Being a fan of fiction means loving stories. Human beings have always been drawn to and persuaded by stories, perhaps more so than any other method of communication. Give statistics about an important issue and you've interested some people; tell a good story and you've attracted a much bigger audience.

The great religious books cherished by humanity are filled with epic stories about what makes a person valuable and how to create a life well lived. Epic stories tell us of sinners and saints, and of the mistakes and the sacrifices they made. When we hear of such adventures, we connect with the people who experienced them. And if you think about it, even in stories based on real life, most of the time the audience does not meet the people featured in the stories, either because they are from the past or live far away. In that sense audiences experience fictional stories and true stories in very similar ways. In other words, our experience of Oskar Schindler (of *Schindler's List*) or of King George IV of England (in *The King's Speech*) is not that different from our experience of Spiderman or Don Draper.

In the world of *Mad Men* fandom, we see the same classic elements that we find in the stories that have been revered and repeated throughout history. Both Aristotle and Joseph Campbell famously wrote about the classic story arc that most popular stories share. They said that stories share a shape and that this shape has common elements, such as a call to action, complications or obstacles, a climax, and some form of resolution.

In a great story we are introduced to characters with whom we can relate emotionally. Those characters then see something that they want or need but cannot have, and we follow them as they find some form of resolution. Sometimes they get what they want, sometimes they don't and determine to go on without it, sometimes they learn that what they thought they wanted was not really what they wanted after all.

Not only do stories naturally draw us in, they also change us. For instance, there are many psychology studies that document how watching a show or reading a story can change your attitude and feelings about the issues and ideas expressed in those stories. *Mad Men*, for example, could take you from never having thought about the ethics of advertising to sharing an opinion on the subject with Peggy's boyfriend Abe, or Midge, the artist and free spirit who was one of Don's mistresses.

A great fictional character doesn't have to be "good" in the moral sense of the word. In fact, great characters are often complex. Don Draper is such a character—already an icon. If your friend says, "I'm getting my Darth Vader on for this meeting," she would be understood. You, likewise, could say, "Don't go all Don Draper on me," and the comment would make sense whether the context suggested serial philandering, chain-smoking, or some other well-known facet of his character.

Don and Peggy certainly don't always (or often?) do the right thing. Yet they have another characteristic necessary for iconic characters — authenticity. You might ask whether there is such a thing as fictional authenticity. We believe there is. For example, Don and Peggy come across as authentic human beings. In part, this comes from the actors: Jon Hamm shows us Don Draper's face; Elisabeth Moss co-creates Peggy for us.

Jon and Elisabeth are real human beings with real emotions, showing us the depth and the reality of their experience. And without going into a treatise on acting theory, actors do feel emotions as they play characters. And we feel real emotions as we watch them.

For instance, when Don proposes to Megan, we might get angry at him for misleading Dr. Faye and for making a rash decision. After all, when Don left town, he had been dating Dr. Faye, and she had no reason to believe he would return home with a fiancée! But when you see the look in Don's eyes as he watches Megan with his kids, you connect with Don's genuine desire for a happy, healthy family.

This authenticity is due to the writers and the production team, who create their world behind the scenes, as well as to the immense talents of the actors. If Jon Hamm were a hack, we wouldn't understand and perhaps we wouldn't care as much that he seems to reach out to Megan, in part, as a way of attempting to provide the children with a warm and caring mother figure.

Now, of course, for some fans Don's motives (and there are always multiple motives swirling in Don's head, it seems) may not be so compelling anyway. Still, what fans expressed most often is not that they can't feel what Don's feeling, but that they are angry at him for his series of misguided choices and behaviors. And in fiction as in real life, the opposite of love isn't hate: it's indifference. Whatever fans decide about Don, they are not indifferent to him.

Whether it's through our consideration of "what if" or through Jon's realistic delivery, or both, we feel a reality to the lives we're watching. If it's true that the opposite of any great truth is another great truth, then perhaps we can also accept that the other side of fiction is reality.

As you will read in these pages, fans do indeed struggle with whether or not Don is a "good" or even redeemable person. They see flashes of humanity—flashes of compassion and even greatness. For instance, when fans watch Don paint Anna Draper's living room or speak lovingly with Sally, they see the good in him. Then at other times, they also feel great disappointment, frustration, even anger and hatred toward Don . . . as when he chastises Megan because, as an actress, she must kiss another man during a performance.

These mixed emotions lead us to wonder. We wonder if Don is a tragic figure, doomed to ultimate failure, and whether or not he will ultimately redeem himself. These are some of the questions the fans ask about Don Draper. More on these questions in the epilogue when we discuss the show's ending . . . the much-anticipated resolution to the long story arc.

In a complex, long-form drama like *Mad Men*, not only is there an overarching story arc (as in what is *Mad Men* "about" or what does *Mad Men* teach us), but there are individual character arcs and a set of themes that unveil themselves as the larger story unfolds. And, in fact, many of these questions will endure, no matter what the conclusion is or how resolved we feel after the "resolution."

As mentioned in chapter 1, some fans speculate that *Mad Men* may be about the American Dream. In the sample we studied, some said they believed that *Mad Men* is about never being satisfied. Still other fans see *Mad Men* as an exploration of gender roles or as a relatively accurate historical piece that educates us about America in the 1960s. Others think the show may be mostly about addiction, about redemption, about how one is undone by tragic flaws, or about substance versus appearance.

In the end, perhaps the multiplicity of what fans think *Mad Men* is "about" is one of its enticing features. While one stereotype of the TV viewer is that of a simpleton digesting fare created to entertain the masses, there's another view of the TV fan represented by *Mad Men* fans. In the world of television today, there is room for niche marketing. Part of the appeal of a complex drama like *Mad Men* is precisely its ambiguity, its paradoxes, and its ability to evoke a host of emotions in the capable viewer.

Karen, the first author of this book, wrote another book about the psychology of media use called *How Fantasy Becomes Reality*. That book first came about after many people from a variety of walks of life told her that when people watch TV or movies, they are completely unchanged by the experience simply because adults know the difference between fantasy and reality. On one level, of course, we are aware that fiction is fiction and that the actor Jon Hamm plays the character Don Draper. Fans have sometimes been shamed for being fans on the grounds that they are out of touch with reality or, at least, that they're spending too much time on something that doesn't matter. We've heard people deride fans for caring about fictional characters at all.

As media psychologists we see that as hypocritical and uninformed. If people didn't really care about the stories they watch — if stories didn't have a truth of their own at some fundamental level — then why would they spend so much of their precious free time connecting with these characters and stories? Why would our interest in them be so intense? Perhaps *it would be* a real sign of pathology if we directed so much energy toward something that was not meaningful . . . something that made no difference in our lives.

We argue that when we're engaged with a fictional story, we are working to understand life better. Engaging with fiction allows us to ask big questions like what makes a good person, what's meaningful in life, and why do people continue to make the same mistakes over and over. Just like any popular story — from the *Arabian Nights* to *Aesop's Fables*, from *Little Red Riding Hood* to the *Wizard of Oz*, *Mad Men* attracts us to its world and leaves us changed from our journey there. This is not because we're misguided but because we're human. And what humans understand better than anything else are stories.

In the next section we move on to discussing how and why fiction plays a role in the formation of our real-life attitudes and beliefs. As we discuss how we identify with characters and stories, we touch upon some possible responses to the age-old question about TV: why do we watch?

Any good storyteller knows that you need engaging characters as well as an interesting story line to attract an audience and capture its collective imagination. One way psychologists who study our connection to fiction talk about our connection to characters is as "identification." Identification means that you feel a bond with the character and can see things from his or her perspective. Once you identify with a character, you can see life through her eyes. You hear her arguments and they make sense (due, of course, in part to these arguments being constructed by brilliant writers).

A well-written argument in a fictional story can get inside your head and your heart, shifting your understanding of a subject toward those characters with whom you've formed a bond. For example, some fans in our research expressed an intense desire to see Don or Peggy "do the right thing," so to speak. They really cared about whether Don or Peggy ever get their lives to a healthy place. Maybe they want Don to stop abusing alcohol or cheating on his lovers. Maybe they want Peggy to see that she's become what she hated when she was younger. We hunger for them to live a good life as we hunger for it ourselves.

It used to be that psychologists defined identification as the degree to which we think a character is "like us." That often meant that a character shared our demographics: sex, religion, race, age, and the like. Then researchers dug deeper and learned that connecting to a fictional character can mean something more. Juan-José Igartua and his colleagues define character identification as having three elements: 1) empathy (feeling what the character feels), 2) imagination (thinking about what it's like to be the character), and 3) merging (feeling like you have become the character).

For example, some viewers feel what Dr. Faye feels as she helps Don through challenging times: we imagine what we'd feel like if, after helping him and becoming invested in the relationship, Don called us and told us he was marrying his secretary; we feel that we are merging with Dr. Faye as she takes the phone call where she gets the shocking news. Together, we feel betrayed, angry, and full of self-doubt. Our heart breaks, and we want to squelch the love we feel for Don, while, at the same time, we grow angry and resentful. (Don Draper, you snake!)

These experiences—empathy, imagination, and merging—are not the signs of a sick mind that can't tell the difference between fantasy and reality but of a healthy and very human mind, a mind where stories entertain and teach us. Because of our minds' abilities to engage with stories, we can use them to ask important questions about life and to have experiences outside of those available in our own limited surroundings.

We believe that our connection to story characters, rather than being a sort of detached identification, is more like an avatar experience. Now, the word "avatar" has a number of different meanings. In today's world, rich with interactive technologies, the most common usage may be that of the human image on a screen connected to a human looking into that screen. These kinds of avatars can be the video game characters we select so that we can play "as" that person or the image that represents us in a virtual reality world or even on a shopping site. You can get an avatar to try on your clothes at an online clothier, decorate your avatar with white hair and green eyes on your Wii (this avatar is your Mii), or even create your own sixties avatar in the *Mad-Men*-Yourself app.

Another use of the term "avatar" is the one used in James Cameron's highly successful film *Avatar*. In this film not only does the avatar whose consciousness the main character, Jake Sully, takes over have a real body, but *his* real body must be in stasis — locked down in a chamber and connected with electrodes and wires — while his mind ventures off to play as the avatar. In *Avatar*, Jake has sustained an injury that took away his ability to walk. When his body goes in the chamber and Jake is connected to his avatar, he can walk, run, swim, and — with the help of a companion creature — even fly as his avatar.

In a very real sense, when a fan connects deeply to a character in a favorite story, the fan is like the body that has been put into stasis while their consciousness experiences life through an avatar. The avatar then is part us (thinking and feeling with our mind) and part character. The mind is strapped in to the roller coaster of the ever-moving story line. In the case of *Mad Men*, we become Don or Sally, Joan or Lane, or any of the characters in the story when we sit down before the screen and get drawn into that universe.

As psychologists we can tell you that the brain actually seems prepared — set up, if you will — to experience the world through connections like this to those we watch. One exciting area of study that's relevant to these connections is the study of mirror neurons — brain cells where other people's actions that we watch are mirrored or reflected. Our mirror neurons seem designed to help us merge with others — to feel what they feel and act as they act. When the human nervous system came into being in roughly its present form, TV hadn't been invented. Of course, like all of our biological systems, the nervous system takes a form that is adaptive — in other words, the nervous system has evolved to help us survive and reproduce. The reason we have a system of mirror neurons, primed for imitation and empathy, is because it is adaptive for us to feel what others feel and to imitate what they do. This is a key way humans learn and empathize. Without these abilities humans wouldn't be humans.

Our current world of immersive storytelling is the result of our attraction to story, our love of sight and sound, and our ability to create amazing technologies. When we sit before the screen and enter our favorite story world, it is as if we have left our body behind — or at least, we've put our own sense of self on the back burner while we merge with the character on the screen and experience life through that person's perspective. Therefore, it should surprise no one that our relationships with our favorite characters and stories are important to us. We feel as though we've lived their lives — experienced their trials and triumphs, felt what it means to be that person. Again, this doesn't mean that we're crazy or out of touch with reality. We're doing what humans were designed to do — empathize with others and vicariously experience the lives we watch them lead.

Some say that when we enter a story world, we willingly suspend our disbelief. For others this is too weak a concept to do justice to the experience. Rather than just deciding that we won't disbelieve, some prefer to say that we can't help but believe what we see.

Perhaps our capacity to make human connections is at the heart of the very meaning of life. If so, then the stories we appreciate help make us who we are, because they allow us to visit times and places we never could otherwise, and meet — and yes, in a sense, even *be* — people whom we could not be in real life.

Think for a moment about the places we go and the people we meet in the *Mad Men* universe. Although they are admittedly, at least at times, much more challenging and exasperating than many of the people we encounter in our daily lives, they are also sharper, more well-defined, more vivid and intriguing than many of the people we meet in real life. In a drama characters are scripted in ways that make their perspective and wit superconcentrated.

Have you ever, for example, known a real man who spouted as many quotable lines as we get from Roger Sterling? Have you ever known a real woman who is as earnest as the young Peggy we meet in the pilot? Or as driven as she becomes as the years go by? And lest we forget, the people in our real lives are unlikely to be as physically attractive or as well-turned-out as our friends in the *Mad Men* universe. If you ever saw a woman on the street as gorgeous as Christina Hendricks, with her unbelievable figure, wearing a ruby-colored vintage dress with matching mani-pedi, how would you really react? (Surely with a gasp and a gape at the very least!) And if you got to see this person at her weakest and strongest moments, as a sinner and as a saint, with stakes as high as those Joan plays with in the *Mad Men* world, well, I imagine you'd never take your eyes off her.

If she were part of your everyday life, Joan Harris would likely be the most compelling figure you'd ever known. And on the show we see Joan beside all the other incredibly attractive and compelling people who make up her world — beside Roger, Don, and Pete, beside Peggy, Betty, Sally, and Megan — each one so vivid and so capable of drawing an emotional response with powers far greater than those of mortal men. We love this sassy fan tribute to the lovely Joan: figure 7 shows the Barbie version of Joan turning heads just like actress Christina Hendricks and Joan herself.

In sum, there are marked differences between the vividness, intensity, and clarity of television and real life. Real life is often more boring, less dramatic, less vivid, less intense, and less clear than fiction. We've heard friends remark that if their life was a reality TV show it wouldn't hold an audience because there would be many scenes where they sit on the sofa or stare at a computer screen.

The great American psychologist William James spoke about how this type of vividness and intensity grabs our attention and emotions. One of the roles of emotion in our lives is to mark events as important. In fact, very emotional experiences create what are called "flashbulb memories," times so vivid that our brains basically take a picture of the moment because our psyches recognize that it is important.

You could make the argument that what we see on television fits the definition of supernormal stimuli. As an example, an apple is a normal sweet food. An Oreo cookie is a supernormal stimulus — more vivid and intense

Figure 7. Barbie Joan turns heads. Photo by Michael Williams/MyLifeInPlastic.com.

than sweets created by Mother Nature. And so too is great TV drama—more intense than life created by Mother Nature. The result is something that provokes us to listen, think, feel, and remember.

In the world of *Mad Men*, we go on a journey where we can imagine and feel what it would have been like to be a young woman like Peggy starting as a secretary at a Manhattan ad agency and then making her way up the corporate ladder—but also living through trying and exhilarating life experiences along the way. In a sense, when we identify with Peggy we become her for a short while, we imagine "what if" we were her, we feel her emotions, and we forget about our lives and who we are as we live and suffer vicariously through her.

Psychologists who study our human connection to story use different words to talk about that process. Currently, a widely used approach is the study of what's called "transportation." Here the word "transportation" is used in the sense of movement, of being moved away from your surroundings and into the story world. When one is transported, your sense of self becomes more remote as your mind travels into the story. Some call this engagement, in the sense of being attached to the story.

Another psychological concept that's used to explain how a fan gets into his or her favorite show or film is called "flow." "Flow" also refers to a state of deep engagement with a subject where one's focus is on that subject to the exclusion of anything else.

Flow is most often associated with the great positive psychologist Mihalyi Csikszentmihalyi (pronounced "Chick sent me high") and is related to Abraham Maslow's concept of the peak experience. For our purposes, both flow and peak experiences share a number of ideas that should resonate with any fan who ever loved a show or franchise. In entering the story world, one loses track of time and feels deeply connected to the experience.

There's also a sense of rightness and joy that the experience has value and meaning. When we watch a favorite story we lose ourselves inside it. And when it's really good, we feel that the ideas the story shares with us are important—important for us and for others—and that spending time with that story has been valuable and meaningful. This is a far cry from the typical notion that watching TV is a mindless waste of time. Of course, not every show is *Mad Men*.

But our link to a story isn't uniform, is it? It isn't black and white. We don't either give up our ego and go into another body *or* stay focused on ourselves and stay in our body. We can move from one perspective to another. We can flit between one character and the next: perhaps we're more attached to Don in one moment than to Betty, or more attached to Peggy now than to Joan. We flit between being the watcher and the watched and then back again. One moment you can feel what Peggy feels; the next you can feel what Don feels; the next you can return to your world and analyze the show from outside its perspective. And that's one thing *Mad Men* fans are known for — analyzing the show. It's to this topic that we turn next.

As noted above, one commenter called *Mad Men* an "exploration of defining meaning as a human being." One could argue that all of fandom is about that — how the particular story helps us understand the human condition. Our argument is that one way of looking at the whole of fandom is that it helps us understand the social world and our place in it. Watching someone else's mistakes and punishments, triumphs and rewards, feelings and motivations helps us understand simultaneously how others feel and act and how we might feel and act in a situation that has similar psychological parameters.

If we move in deeper we can see that there are many facets to the explorations we do when watching others in this intense and vivid dramatic context. As noted: our perspective as a viewer is not static. Our minds are imagining all kinds of different perspectives and ideas very quickly. We are able to explore a novel situation while also finding commonalities in the situation with our own experience. Some psychologists argue that all learning really takes place this way — by associating something novel with something we already know. And, of course, viewer perspectives differ too because individual experience differs: what is novel to one viewer is not novel to another. Now layer on top of that the idea that we're also able to jump from avatar to avatar as the characters perform their social dance on the screen, moving from center stage to periphery to off-screen as we watch.

Keep in mind that we're also able to cut back to yet another perspective — that of a meta-analytic view of the show as a show that is written, produced, and dramatized by a staff of people. This brings to mind again the stereotype that being a TV fan is necessarily passive and mindless. In fact, the viewer who is lost in the story is actively engaged in relatively complex processing: thinking, feeling, analyzing, and switching perspectives. On top of that, almost definitional of a complex drama like *Mad Men* is an ambiguous nature, which, in turn, can leave fans not knowing what to conclude.

In the case of *Mad Men*, we watch Don in an attempt to understand what makes him happy, what gives him meaning, what is a good decision in his world. We get frustrated because he makes so many bad decisions. We wonder whether or not he'll ever get it right. We also ask if any of the other characters have figured life out. Do they know what makes them happy? What gives them a sense of meaning? Do they treat the people around them well? If they are immoral or amoral, do their motives make sense? We ask these things not because we think we'll have a crack at Madison Avenue in the 1960s ourselves but because these are universal questions. Each of us has but one life, and that's not enough. It's not enough experience to prepare us to make the best choices.

Through stories we gain the ability to experience life as other people in other places and other times. Men can feel what it's like to be a woman. Kids can feel what it's like to be their parents' or grandparents' age. Plain people can feel something of what it's like to be attractive. Isn't that part of what we mean when we say that fictional stories are an escape from our realities? We may not have had Peggy's job in that place and time, but we've worked with other people, we've lived through situations with similar emotional and psychological meanings. And so we can easily feel what she's feeling and think about what we'd like to see her do to resolve her issues.

Over the long arc of the story, as fans we spend so much time going where Peggy goes, feeling what she feels, and wrestling with the decisions she makes that we have merged with her. Meanwhile, another facet of great storytelling is in play. This facet lies in the writer's trick of giving us enough conflict and uncertainty that it keeps us coming back for more. When Ted leaves Peggy, it bothers many of us and we want that resolved. Sometimes that need for resolution manifests itself in fans writing stories where Ted and Peggy get together and live happily ever after. This is a kind of fan dream — a Freudian wish fulfillment in which what is most important to us on the show yet remains unresolved and so is resolved by other means.

Other fans don't write fan fiction, but they blog or they comment on other people's blogs. In this way fans can share their emotions and desires. They can express their joy at a good father-daughter moment between Don and Sally. They can discuss their disgust with Don as a romantic partner when he has, yet again, cheated on a wife or lover. Through our exposure to other fans' stories and discussions, we see that the show matters to other people — not just to us.

What we learn from stories isn't always simple or straightforward. Have you ever come away from *Mad Men* feeling that what you just experienced touched upon something grand, something larger than you or even the show? Great storytelling moves us in this way. We need not always emerge with a clear lesson.

In fact, it's common when appreciating a work of art to find the greatest value in experiences that evoke mixed emotions. According to our data on the fan experience, *Mad Men* often leaves fans with these kinds of compelling mixed feelings. We feel love and hate for a character, derision and pity, joy and sorrow — these feelings can signal that the story is important to us, as they are signals in our own real-life experiences.

Mixed emotions are not the only complexities we fans value in our stories. In fact, storytellers have known for a long time that the desire for resolution is more complex than meets the eye. Music fans may know that, to the human ear, an unresolved musical line provokes the listener to long for the musical resolution of that line. Likewise, a story without an ending produces the desire for a resolution.

A writer who understands human psychology knows that the audience wants to have unresolved issues addressed. But the writer may believe that giving too much resolution will negate the need of the audience to keep coming back for more. So writers may resolve bits of an issue while still leaving the door open to unknowns in order to hold the attention of the audience. As you'll see in the fan comments from our research, *Mad Men* fans do sit on the edge of their seats, wishing and hoping that the show's characters will do the right thing, get it together, make good, come out victorious.

As they do this, they keep coming back for more. So, this is another reason fans watch — to get that taste of resolution from problems presented in the past. Conflict, inherent in storytelling, is one specific reason we keep coming back to watch a show again and again — to see how it is resolved. Of course, as we watch, the writers introduce more plot points and more conflicts that beg for resolution. Fans find themselves addicted to a story that offers some form of resolution but continues to raise new questions.

This longing for resolution is in operation week to week and season to season on television shows. It is also in operation in relation to the grand story arc. Do you remember the buttons that characters wore in the film *The Truman Show* that read "How will it end?" That's essentially the question fans asked as they watched *Mad Men*. Would the ending involve Don's suicide or redemption? And what of Peggy? Would she return to her core values, or was she essentially a female Don, scraping and clawing her way to the top? How would our Peggy "turn out"? Was Megan, as some fans proposed, Sharon Tate? And what about Sally? Obviously Don, Betty, Megan, and the rest gave Sally ample fodder for the therapy couch in later years, but would she find a way to thrive despite her upbringing? Would Don and Betty ultimately have scarred their own child irrevocably, just as they were scarred? What will the legacy of the show be to us and to the culture?

And now, to learn more about how fans make sense of *Mad Men* as a period piece, we move on to the next chapter, "That Was Then, This Is Now."

CHAPTER THREE

That Was Then, This Is Now

It was the age of Betty Friedan, where social issues, relationships, and roles were shifting and being redefined. The turbulent and innovative sixties are the cultural landscape that *Mad Men* explores through the efforts of its characters to grapple with the cultural change. Historical events, from the assassination of John F. Kennedy to the liftoff of the moon-bound Apollo 11 spacecraft, occur during the show, but even more important to the people of *Mad Men* are the significant changes underway in women's work and relationships between men and women. Fans love to compare and contrast contemporary life to the times represented in *Mad Men* and to find inconsistencies between the show's portrayal of the 1960s and what they think really happened.

In this chapter we will explore how fans engage with and make meaning of *Mad Men*'s representation of historical events, behaviors, roles, and relationships. Using the data we collected from *Mad Men* fans' online-forum conversations, we take a close look at fans' views on what has changed and what has stayed the same.

Popular Memory

Events, social movements, and environments become part of our popular memory, and popular media like television often help shape that consciousness. The story of *Mad Men* allows us to peer into a vision of the sixties in the United States that concentrates on members of the affluent middle class in and around New York City. With painstaking accuracy and attention to detail, show runner Matthew Weiner paints a backdrop so emotionally evocative of the decade that the viewer senses and feels more than knows the period.

From set-design details to the clothing worn by the characters, everything is historically accurate. And when there is a mistake in the accuracy, *Mad Men* fans call it out — some make a hobby of it. From the wrong brand of beer to the yellowed (signs of aging) plastic piece on the IBM typewriter (how could a brand-new-on-the-scene product show signs of aging?), *Mad Men* fans find it. For example, in season one Don Draper is at home drinking beer after beer. The beer is Fielding beer. Fielding beer wasn't around back then. And boy did the fans let the producers of *Mad Men* know it.

Another notable gaffe was Peggy's telephone. As a fan pointed out, "Peggy has a telephone (with some sort of strange finger-holed wheel) in a kicky, girlish yellow. But it's so unrealistic! A working girl would never splurge her meager salary on such fripperies — 'vanity' phones cost extra in the bad old days when Ma Bell was a raging alcoholic control freak. And Peggy's not vain!" Fans notice whether magazines and newspapers show the correct dates and take note of vintage office Rolodex cards. One fan found the Drapers' kitchen to be not up to snuff: "While the office look was quite good, the Drapers' kitchen was a bit too off. That 1948/49 GE refrigerator was way too old for them. It made no sense to have a pale yellow wall oven that DIDN'T match the fridge or the electric cook top."

Nor is the soundtrack off limits; one fan discovered that the background music playing in a Japanese restaurant featured on the show hadn't been released yet. Great sleuthing. The ultimate probably came when Brian Williams put Matthew Weiner in the hot seat during a cast interview for *NBC Nightly News*. The anchorman pointed out that Joan Harris's throwaway line about making a reservation at Le Cirque was an anachronism — *Mad Men* was set in 1968 in that episode, and the famed New York restaurant didn't open until 1974. Others target the narrow slice of society that the show focuses on: "As I watched last night's episode draw to a close," one fan wrote, "I was kind of annoyed. Life was not like that for everybody who grew up during those years. Or got married during those years. Or who started careers during those years. Or whatever."

But the show's characters aren't designed to be actual historical figures. Instead, they appear to exist in order to allow us, the viewers, to have a window into the sixties and early seventies. Some fans think that *Mad Men* is not so much about what happens during an episode but rather about the transformation of its characters as they move through life. In this sense the time period is less important than universal human themes.

As we watch an episode of *Mad Men*, looking for accuracies or whether the story line rings true, we activate our memory and emotions, and the deeper the emotions run the more meaningful the episode can be to us. Because Matthew Weiner and his team spent the time to set the stage so well with period details, the viewer can easily be drawn into the story and disengage from scanning for accuracy. *Mad Men* fans often engage with the sense and feel of the story, becoming so immersed in the story that cultural time frames become fluid. This example can be seen in the following fan quote, where the focus is on the human emotion of the moment: "One thing that has stood out watching *Mad Men* is how important demeanor is over content, you can pretty well take any line that another male character says and switch it with one of Don's, and by and large, all things would be equal. The communication is all in the delivery, or non-delivery, as when nothing needs to be said, there's no reason to say it."

Nevertheless, as one fan reminds us, a show looking back at a real time period cannot help but be part of our shared dream world and a construction of our popular memory. Is it real? Is it realistic? We can check show content against historical records for accuracy (Matthew Weiner has been praised for his attention to detail here). The fan argues that, despite all the care and consideration by the show's creator to truthfully represent the time period, some might sense a bit of a disconnect between historical detail and our popular memory of the time: feel versus fact. This fan argues, "What is really spectacular about it is the tension between it being spectacularly well observed and being like the fantasy of an advert world: it's a programme just as much about how advertising and dreaming has distorted our understanding of the 50s and 60s as it is brilliantly, perfectly observed."

Fans love the nostalgia of the show. They often see the sixties as a better time, a time of hope, and a time when Americans were optimistic and expected successful, happy lives and new horizons. One fan begged, "Please transport me back to the 1960s." However historically accurate such views may be, research supports the idea that nostalgia may make people more optimistic about the future and play a beneficial role in people's lives. And not only can engaging in nostalgia provide a nice balance to your emotions but it can also aid in fighting loneliness and boredom and giving you a greater sense of purpose and connection. As a result, it can even reduce mortality.

Popular media researcher Lynn Spigel conducted a survey on contemporary people's views of women in the fifties, asking the participants how they thought of the past. Two behaviors emerged: comparison and familiarization through engaging with images. *Mad Men* fans are offered both. Thanks to the evocative stage setting and the actors that Matthew Weiner has painstakingly created, fans are able to engage with images to make meaning and compare what was then and what is now. Together emotions and reason can influence how much we engage. *Mad Men* gives us the opportunity to poke fun at outdated social roles and norms while also enjoying the nostalgia, possibly tickling our own sweet memories of the time. Doing so engages both our emotional and logical sides. We can fantasize about living in the *Mad Men* era, even dream of skinny ties, pencil skirts, whiskey drinks, and too many cigarettes.

Yet, as psychologists, we know that every act of remembering can change our memories. We still do not have a definitive understanding of why we hang on to some bits of information and events and not others. We do know that flashbulb memory is linked to unique and highly emotional events (such as the assassination of John F. Kennedy or the Apollo 11 mission) and that such memories are more vulnerable to alteration as we play them over and over again in our minds, have conversations about the event, and engage in stories about the event. We are then left with a new version of truth. So when a fan says that *Mad Men* is "a pretty accurate portrait of early 60's middle-class men by all accounts. I wish I'd been around then," we realize that this memory is a synthesis of invention, environment, and remembering.

Social Critique

Other fans are less sentimental and look back on the decade with a negative lens, calling it out as a period dominated by privileged white men. In particular, *Mad Men* juxtaposes rampant sexism alongside feminist awakening but doesn't quite confront the era's racism. Otis Moss from the *Daily Beast*

Figure 8. Employees at Sterling Cooper gather around the television (along with the whole country), watching in horror as the events of the Kennedy assassination unfold. Season three, episode twelve, "The Grown-Ups."

describes the scenario this way: "Men, patriarchal and white, are framed as privileged, arrogant, and unaware of the offense and power they wield. They hold power and injure all who come into their view, not with overt malice, but adolescent ignorance. Women are objects of desire and reluctant partners, while black people are invisible to all who live with unannounced privilege."

In depicting the inequalities and other social ills of the 1960s, *Mad Men* allows the fans to consider their personal history, their roles in the past, and the progress made (if any) by comparing the current day to the period portrayed in the series.

The cultural landscape of the sixties as represented in *Mad Men* provides a forum for fans to explore the past and think about how we have evolved, often priding ourselves on how much we have transformed. "I mean, granting that this is a drama, not a documentary, and that people are hard to categorize," one fan wrote, "I'd say we live healthier now, we are more aware of how to combat addictions and we make more of an effort to have healthy relationships with the people closest us. Also, much less with the racism/sexism thing: whatever one might say about those issues in contemporary society, no one's hiding the black employees or telling a woman that technology is so simple 'even a woman can operate it.'"

Indeed, the difficulties women faced at home and at work in this era are a major theme of the show, as our analysis of fans' fascination with Peggy, Joan, Betty, and the other major female characters shows (detailed in chapter 5). Betty's unhappy marriage to Don provides an especially painful example of the social and legal limits women faced: "Try imagining being this woman who was an international model with a degree in Anthropology (not an easy A) at Bryn Mawr," one fan wrote. "She could have had a way more exciting life than being a stay at home wife and mother of three. So excuse her if she pouts every now and then and takes her dissatisfaction out on her kids for limiting her life" in season three.

Betty's plight — and her very name — might have been designed to evoke the best-known feminist critic of the 1960s, Betty Friedan. In her famous book *The Feminine Mystique*, she wrote, "Each suburban wife struggles with it alone. As she made the beds, shopped for groceries, matched slipcover material, ate peanut butter sandwiches with her children, chauffeured Cub Scouts and Brownies, lay beside her husband at night — she was afraid to ask even of herself the silent question — 'Is this all?'"

Fans also take an interest in changing ideals of parenting. While some parental restrictions were tougher in *Mad Men* days, in some cases children had more freedom than they often do now. For example, the daughter of a sixties ad man that we spoke to said that it was not unusual for her at age ten to take the train with a friend into New York City to shop or go to Madison Square Garden. A fan shared, "I think that the Betty character is not too far off from the accepted parenting practices of the time. The prevailing methods were very hands off and punitive." Another fan confirmed that perspectives and cultural values placed on parenting have shifted, warning other fans, "Do not get hung up applying 21st century axioms and political correctness on 1960's life style. As information and knowledge became more reliable and accessible, life styles changed. What is considered as 'bad mothering' in 2010 was acceptable in 1960. Betty Draper, while having her faults, was a personification of the times. Just look at how all the women, men, & parents act on *Mad Men*, pregnant or not."

Frequently fans express unhappiness about how race is portrayed on *Mad Men* and how the characters on *Mad Men* deal with issues of race. In season three Pete Campbell is tasked with finding a new campaign strategy for the Admiral Television account. The brand has poor sales and is struggling to stay afloat. Pete comes up with a brilliant idea to pitch Admiral televisions to black markets, where he sees strong sales, cities such as Oakland, Chicago, Washington, D.C., and Kansas City. The full media campaign would include ads in black newspapers and *Ebony* magazine. Pete is quickly shut down when partner Bert Cooper fumes, "Admiral Television has no interest in becoming a colored television company."

What's worse is that fans agree that the racism depicted on the show is fairly accurate for the period. Showing the pervasive racism of the 1960s on *Mad Men* provides a platform for discussion and checking in on how much or whether we are better now. Black characters at Sterling Cooper Draper Pryce are often invisible and overlooked. (Remember the black janitor who observed the Peggy/Pete tryst or the opening scene of *Mad Men* when Don is speaking with an African-American bar employee but interrupted by the white manager apologizing for the server?)

In one *Mad Men* episode Peggy's "girl" Shirley receives flowers from her fiancé. Assuming the flowers are a gift to Peggy from Ted, Peggy snatches the flowers off Shirley's desk, never giving it a thought that the flowers might actually belong to Shirley. In the same episode the black secretary Dawn is subjected to ad agency partner Lou Avery's tirade and insults, shuffled around like a pawn being reassigned (but not fired because, as Avery states, they can't).

Responding to these characters, one fan wrote, "The whole thing with Dawn & Shirley was awful . . . and so true of the times. Not just because they are black, but also because they are women . . . disposable, easily interchanged. Bert broke my heart too."

But white men don't exactly have it easy on the show, either. Although they hold most of the power, many of the male characters and the masculine norms of the 1960s prevent them from building satisfying lives — none more so than Don Draper himself. (We have more to say about this in chapter 6.) Laughingly, actor Jon Hamm pokes fun at fans who approach him and say that they want to be just like Don Draper. "Really?" he asks. "You want to be a miserable drunk? You want to be like the guy on the poster, maybe, but not the actual guy. The outside looks great, the inside is rotten. That's advertising. Put some Vaseline on that food, make it shine and look good. Can't eat it, but it looks good."

Let's face it, Don Draper looks pretty darn good on the surface. Throw in some tailored suits, nice digs, gorgeous women, and winning ad campaigns, and the image only looks better. Compare that against the sad and constant womanizing, broken marriage(s?), horrible childhood, using an alias name and always concerned it will be discovered, and the list continues. He is a broken man with a shiny exterior — perhaps an allegory for the 1960s themselves.

The same could be said about the imagined glamour of the *Mad Men*-style cocktail parties. This fan's ironic comment perfectly captures the shadows behind the fabulous events: "Ah, the days of the Mad-Men Cocktail Parties. Of course they were held before the facts of drinking too much, or what driving home from the party can end up costing. The chain smoking party goers aren't so glamorous today, as they stroll along with their oxygen tanks, or most likely 6 ft. under." The fan admits, "I too love this old Vintage lifestyle of days gone by. Unfortunately, they are just that, Days gone By. As much as I like this concept, to engage in one of these parties, has consequences. I honestly do not know anyone wanting to drink martini's, eat cheese balls, jello, deviled eggs, pigs in a blanket and cupcakes. All loaded with Carbs. Different day, time and era, that one can never go back." Except "maybe on Halloween." And that's our next topic: how fans incorporate the show into their lives.

Fan Activities

As we show throughout this book, *Mad Men* fans deeply connect with the times and identify with the characters. They ask themselves, what if I were in that situation, what might I say? And fans do put themselves in the shoes of a character they sympathize with — sometimes quite literally. One of the ways fans bring the show into their own lives is by recreating some of the activities that are so popularly shown on the show. From *Mad Men* cocktail recipes to themed vacation tours, fans are acting out being *Mad Men* themselves. We are social or, as is often said, highly social animals. We like to connect and be a part of a group, and the Internet makes it easy to form *Mad Men* fan groups, connect, and have a fan-based identity. It is not uncommon to want to be a part of many social groups, and each one requires a tweak in our identity. Our group affiliation guides our behavior, so dressing, drinking, and playing like *Mad Men* characters allows us to connect with other *Mad Men* fans and also subconsciously to reinforce our identity as, perhaps, a suave, sexy, and successful, if a tad bit arrogant, businessman (aka Don Draper). Or maybe we'd rather be a curvaceous, sensual, and competitive office manager/ company partner characterized by what one fan calls "uber-womanness" (aka Joan Holloway).

Or we'd like to emulate a woman who succeeds in breaking tradition and successfully rising above sexist expectations, thanks to her staunch determination to thrive in a male-dominated working world (aka Peggy). Then again, maybe it's more fun to imagine ourselves as an affluent, spoiled, naggingly insecure mad man (aka Pete). Dressing up allows us to don their allure (pun intended) without all the risks (wife finding out we've visited the brothel) or try on a new identity that can inspire us to become more like what we'd like to be. In that sense playing a fictional character isn't so different from joining a prestigious athletic club and starting to eat healthy (or at least having a green juice at the health club bar).

During our research we were able to speak with a daughter of an actual *Mad Men*. Her father worked on Madison Avenue in advertising, and she grew up in Ossining in Westchester County, New York, the same location where Don Draper and his wife Betty started raising a family. She explained that there was a distinction in *Mad Men* style. The creative ones, the ones downstairs, were able to get away with facial hair and bell-bottoms and dressing the part (turtle neck, pipe, tweed jacket with suede patches at the elbow). On the other hand, the executives upstairs wore the suit and tie and had short hair. Dress was important in the sixties. It made a statement about the major social shifts underway. This reality is even played out with the *Mad Men* characters when Joan Holloway scolds Peggy: "You want to be taken seriously. Stop dressing like a little girl."

Bloggers Tom & Lorenzo have run a decade-old blog primarily focused on the show's fashion, and they have a dedicated following. The two are major devotees of Janie Bryant, the *Mad Men* costume designer, singing her praises for her attention to detail and period authenticity. They recap each episode of *Mad Men* with a highly detailed look at the fashion. *Mad Men* fans love it. "*Mad Men*'s costuming is brilliant!" is a usual *Mad Men* fan shout-out. The *Mad Men* cultural fashion phenomenon has even boosted sales of skinny ties and pomade.

The *Mad Men*–inspired vintage sixties-look clothing collection that Banana Republic has sold for several seasons has led *Mad Men* fans to compare the contemporary garments to what they used to wear or what they remember being worn, just as they compare the show's portrayal of the sixties to their own experiences or knowledge. "This is a very cute collection," one fan wrote. "Nice interpretation of the mid-to late '60's looks. I especially love the shoes. I had little heels like those when I was in high school." "My aunt, who is only seven years older than I, was in high school during this time and that's exactly how she dressed," another remembered. "She was so groovy." Both fans offered fond positive memories that they are now able to recreate if they want to by buying these clothes.

Banana Republic did not stop at the *Man Men* collection. The fashion retail chain took bolder steps to engage the fans and extend the *Mad Men* fashion as a hot theme. They partnered with Virgin America for an in-flight fashion show at 35,000 feet, oh my! Banana Republic also partnered with AMC for two seasons to offer an episode walk-on role for fans of *Mad Men* dressed in an outfit from the Banana Republic *Mad Men* collection. Customers voted for their favorite photo. In the second year's casting call (for season five) Matthew Weiner made the final selection, choosing two winners. Fans love participating—dressing up and congratulating the winner. One fan wrote to one winner, "Great choice! This picture looks like a scene from 'Mad Men' itself. It makes you want to know who this person is and what her story might be. An old friend of Joan's contemplating a little blackmail and providing us with much desired information on Joan's history, as well? Congratulations to you, Amy, a well deserved win. I hope your 'Mad Men' role is more than just a walk-on."

Fans' attraction to *Mad Men*–era sixties design doesn't stop at fashion. Viewers are also drawn to vintage or vintage-inspired furniture. *Elle Décor* features a spread on its favorite design elements from the midtown Man-hattan offices that Sterling Cooper Draper Pryce occupied for a time. Like the costuming, the show's period design has been called both sumptuous and obsessively fastidious. Nothing is left to chance. *Mad Men* set decora-tor, Claudette Didul-Mann, said, "My father worked in advertising for over 40 years and there was Herman Miller and Knoll furniture everywhere you went." Fans noticed — and now they often seek to locate a piece. Trying to bring a bit of the nostalgia into his home, a fan thanked web site *Mad Men* furniture curators by saying, "I absolutely love the furniture on *Mad Men*, thank you for featuring the furniture and set designers on your site. I am very interested in a reproduction of the coffee table in Don's office in season four, episode seven."

If they can't buy it, fans make it. Etsy, an online place to buy and sell all things homemade, features an eclectic mix of goods such as print art, jewelry, coloring books, and even tarot cards, fan created and *Man Men* inspired. One *Mad Men*–inspired fashion piece received 1007 comments on the single style. Items include, but are certainly not limited to, a Peggy Olson necklace from KitschBitchJewellry, a Joan Holloway laptop decal, a Don Draper fin-ger puppet, and collections of *Mad Men* coloring books. Along more tradi-tional lines but still creative, there are phone covers, vintage *Mad Men* wall art, and "What would [insert *Mad Men* character] do?" prints. Our personal favorite, though, is the *Mad Men* tarot card deck adorned with Joan, Peggy, Betty, Don, Pete, and Roger.

Mad Men fan boards on the social-media web site Pinterest have every-thing from *Mad Men* kits (couch, red lipstick, Lucky Strike cigarettes, type-writer, rotary-dial phone, briefcase, and, of course, a glass of whiskey), character poster art, and ad art to character profile sheets for each major character's favorite app, gadget choice, tech choice, style, social media, and Facebook engagement. True to style Don Draper's reads — "Fave APP, Singles Around Me; Gadget Choice, e-cigarette; Style, The Glenlivet Scotch; Tech Choice, iPad; Social Media, Don doesn't do Social Media, he lives his life off the grid; Facebook Engagement, Don doesn't manage his Fanpage, 'What would Don Draper do?'"

And, of course, the true pièce de résistance, the sign that this fandom has become iconic, Mattel released a *Mad Men* series of Barbie dolls sporting characters Don Draper, Betty Draper, Joan Holloway, and Roger Sterling dolls.

Dressing up and accessorizing are just one way that people re-create the show in real life. Not surprisingly, fan re-creations include drinking sixties-style drinks with sixties-style barware, something AMC has encouraged by posting cocktail recipes on its web site. There's also a *Mad Men* cocktail book and a *Mad Men* cookbook. Fans can watch an episode drinking along with the characters. Think Don Draper sitting in a bar in the opening scene, having an old-fashioned, "Do this again — old-fashioned, please."

At work, during lunch, at home, we see the *Mad Men* characters drinking. A scotch in the office during the day with a client to celebrate, a pour of whiskey to take the edge off and prepare for the first meeting, the three-martini lunch, and, of course, there are evening cocktails as well.

> ROGER STERLING: I bet daily friendship with that bottle attracts
> more people to advertising than any salary you could dream of.
> DON DRAPER: That's why I got in.
> ROGER STERLING: So enjoy it.
> DON DRAPER: [drinks] I'm doing my best here.
> ROGER STERLING: [scoffs] No, you're not. You don't know how
> to drink. Your whole generation, you drink for the wrong reasons.
> My generation we drink because it's good. Because it feels better
> than unbuttoning your collar. Because we deserve it. We drink
> because it's what men do.
> — Season one, episode four, "New Amsterdam."

Fans reminisce, evaluate, disagree, and grapple with the drinking on *Mad Men* and then have a whole lot of fun making drinks, sharing drink recipes, and having cocktail parties all themed around *Mad Men*. They discuss the cultural shift of acceptance and support for drinking on the job. Many fans specifically wrote to say that the three-martini lunch was not an urban legend. As one fan puts it, "It is not unbelievable. *Mad Men* represents the prevailing corporate culture at the time in the U.S. — my father would have three martinis at lunch, work productively until four-thirty, and then start the drinks again. He had crystal old fashioned glasses, an insulated ice bucket, a bottle of scotch, a bottle of bourbon, and a bottle of vodka—in his office."

We are reminded that the *Mad Men* time period was a time when people were socially less straitlaced about drinking in general and on the job. A viewer not only confirmed the prevalence of drinking, he also spoke of the expectations. If you didn't drink, it was an issue. "I'd say the show does have a fairly realistic picture of office attitudes to drinking for the time: a senior ad man is expected to knock back a certain number of drinks per day—and not to do so, like Duck when he's on the wagon, is seen as strange—but if like Freddy you let it interfere with your performance in public, then you're out on your ear."

But now back to the whiskey shortage. Yes, whiskey shortage. Demand is outpacing supply, and some point to *Mad Men* for making whiskey drinks so popular again. As a fan says to the whiskey scarcity, "This is all *Mad Men's* fault." The Manhattan is again a culturally iconic drink. There are bars with fifteen different kinds of Manhattans.

A variety of big cook/chef/caterers (aka Martha Stewart) have thrown their hats into the ring for how to throw the perfect *Mad Men* cocktail party. Martha's web site offers "How to Plan a *Mad Men* Premiere Party," complete with bar setup, party decor, the recipes for the perfect Manhattan and martini, instructions on essential party appetizers—pigs in a blanket and shrimp cocktail. Other retro party ideas for *Mad Men* watchers include serving pickled deviled eggs, gin-marinated olives, and gin-and-tonic Jell-O molds. Epicurious, tongue in cheek, offers the ingredients for a *Mad Men* party: "Some '60s furniture and clothing, cigarettes, booze. To prepare for this party: Buy a vintage suit or dress, drink too much, and practice your sexism." One fan chimed in, "They forgot the celery filled with cheese/pineapple spread."

Mad Men–themed cocktail parties are a popular fund-raising event. The Historical Society of Pennsylvania hosted a *Mad Men* cocktail party, asking members to "Don" their best *Mad Men* attire and get a look at midcentury advertisements while they sipped classic cocktails and ate period hors d'oeuvres.

Fans of *Mad Men* know that in every episode there will be plenty of imbibing. So it is only natural that *Mad Men* drinking games abound, and the series has gotten the nickname of *Drunk Men*. The goal is to enjoy the show, getting as drunk as you can without being as unfortunate as Roger Sterling after his oyster lunch in season one, "The Stairs" (lost his lunch, oysters and all, on the office carpet in front of prospective clients).

The Mad Men Season 5 Drinking Game has participants taking a sip of alcohol when Peggy Olson gets "frustrated with being a working woman" or Pete Campbell acts like a weasel; drinking a shot "whenever Don Draper tells someone, 'No'" or "whenever Betty is a terrible mother"; guzzling the whole cocktail if "there's a Dick Whitman reference" or "Don seduces someone"; downing the whole bottle "if Don and Joan hook up" or "Harry Crane ISN'T a total douche"; and finally switching to a sip of prune juice for every roommate who doesn't watch *Mad Men*. Other seasons have similar versions of the game, switching out a few behaviors that more closely align with the plot for the season and some variation of the nonalcoholic prune juice (such as coffee or herbal tea).

Other drinking games include an iPhone app challenging users to make the perfect *Mad Men* drink and Drinking Cinema, a web site–published game, offering players fun instructions such as "drink whenever you see Knoll furniture" or "drink whenever you see mid-century underwear (e.g., bras, boxers, pantyhose, garters)."

For fans for whom watching the show on TV isn't enough, *Mad Men* tours (walk around Manhattan and visit the iconic *Mad Men* sites) and *Mad Men* vacations have become quite popular, allowing fans to experience the mystique of *Mad Men* while physically being part of the locale.

Given a 100 percent satisfaction on TripAdvisor and ranked 111 of 1,014 for activities in New York City, the Mad Men Cocktail Tour gives fans a chance to drink in (pun intended) the feel of the city (New York City) through the eyes of a *Mad Men* character. Tour guides encourage folks to come dressed as their favorite character or dressed in their best sixties attire as they visit bars featured on the show and iconic advertising landmarks. Fans rave about being able to experience Madison Avenue through the eyes of Roger and Don — albeit with "slightly blurred vision" (how realistic). One fan described how much fun it was to engage with others around their love of *Mad Men*. "We started the tour by meeting our knowledgeable guide Josh at Grand Central station along with another British couple. We visited the snug in the famous Oyster bar at the station for our first potent cocktail and watched scenes from the show—I had a gin fizz which was wonderful!" Next, the small group moved on "to the fabulous Roosevelt hotel where we ordered more cocktails—I'd definitely recommend the martini in here!" Exiting the bar, "we walked along Madison Avenue and learned more about the ad industry and visited the site that Sterling Cooper would have had their offices before ending our tour at PJ Clarkes. This was my favourite bar as there was a real buzz and their Manhattan cocktails were really good!"

As you might guess from the cocktail consumption, "the three hour tour flew by in a blur of fun, facts, lively discussion and theories about the show and of course cocktails! I'd recommend that you wear comfortable shoes for walking between the locations and definitely dress to impress in 1960s attire."

The television series has boosted tourism in Connecticut as well. The state tourism board touts New Canaan, Connecticut (even though Ossining, New York, is where the Drapers lived) as the quintessential *Mad Men* suburban town, the perfect place for *Mad Men* fans to have a Lucky Strike cocktail at the Elm Restaurant. No joke, the Lucky Strike cocktail includes a garnish of ash on top! Of course, fans can also travel to Ossining, New York, and take its *Mad Men* places tour that covers both real and fictional Ossining locations featured on the show.

Other locations advertise *Mad Men* tours, either by linking to direct references in the show or by promising the sense and feel of the same time period. Lakeland, Florida, promotes *Mad Men* vacations with its vintage sixties clothing shops, old movie theatre, vintage soda fountain, and Frank Lloyd Wright architecture. The Retro Cocktail Getaway offers a stay at the Hotel Deluxe in Portland, Oregon, with a hands-on class in the art of *Mad Men*-era cocktails. And the Waldorf Astoria in New York City is considered the quintessential *Mad Men* experience hotel, since it's located in the epicenter of New York City and was featured in season four when Don Draper was working with Conrad Hilton.

And then there are the apps. We mentioned the Mad Men Cocktail Culture app above; it is a recipe guide and a game. The app not only includes

Figure 9. Sally Draper making cocktails for her father. Season two, episode four, "Three Sundays."

drinks to prepare and a cocktail guide but also feedback on your bartending skills. How do your cocktail skills compare with Sally Draper's? Remember, Don had her make a Tom Collins when company was visiting.

The iPhone app Tidbit Trivia for Mad Men — Unofficial Fan App lets fans test themselves to see if they can pass muster as a *Mad Men* expert (and go a bit rogue too with an "unofficial fan" app). "Lee Garner Sr. is the owner of which company that is a client of Sterling Cooper?" Mohawk Airlines? Lucky Strike? Heinz? Kodak? Do you know?

Probably the most fun is the app that will let you *MadMen* Yourself. With the app you can create a *Mad Men*-inspired avatar that you can then use as your profile image for all your social media accounts. You can transform yourself, complete with story line, mood, and authentic period details such as cigarettes, bow ties, scarves, and cocktails. You can download a headshot or a body shot or put your avatar in a *Mad Men* scene. Role-playing without the hangover — though at least one fan wrote, "I wish I were as drunk and groovy as my doppelganger." Another commented, "Wow, I had way too much fun with this. And discovered that, 1) no 60's outfits would flatter my figure, 2) I absolutely love getting drunk while reading the paper and 3) I kind of wish I still smoked."

For one fan creating the *Mad Men* avatar reminded her of her grandmother: "omg i am LOVING this—especially since I actually have one of those silver pencil-on-a-chain necklaces! it was my grandmothers and I wear it ALL THE TIME :)" Others used the app to comment on the show's limits. Addressing the lack of or invisibility of blacks in the *Mad Men* office, a fan said, after creating her avatar and placing it in a *Mad Men* scene, "Hey look! A black person working at Sterling Cooper!"

CHAPTER FOUR

The (Re)Arrangements: Engaging with
Mad Men Through Fan Fiction

Ted smiled and went on his knees; he took her hand and kissed it
gently. "Peggy, I want to marry you. But I know you, I know what your
career means to you. . . . I'd love to get married to you tonight and be
in Hawaii for our honeymoon, but if you got this promotion after we
married that's all people would talk about. You have earned this, and
I don't want to take that away from you. We will get married . . ." Ted
kissed her hand again, "That is, if you'll have me."
— from *Waking Light* by TedChaoughFeelings

Remember the scene above where, after Ted moves back to New York from
California, he offers Peggy a partnership in the advertising agency and asks
her to marry him all at the same time? What about the time Peggy and Don
hooked up? Or Peggy and Joan? Joan and Lane? No, you didn't miss a really
juicy episode of *Mad Men*. These are all things that happened in fan fiction:
stories written by fans that take place in the *Mad Men* universe. As one fan-
fiction writer told us, "I refuse to passively have content put in my head without engaging and 'talking back' with it." Fan fiction (aka fan fic) enables fans
to do just that. In the same way that other fans discuss the show with their
friends or post their thoughts to online message boards, fan-fiction writers
are responding to the show too — they just do so by writing *Mad Men* stories
of their own.

Fan fiction is a creative outlet that lets fans do things like explore the
show's story lines in more detail, reshape and reimagine the characters and
their relationships, and grapple with all the things that go unsaid in the series.
Because fan fiction is a form of audience response different and distinct from

the online discussions we talk about in other chapters, it helps us explore some interesting things like the relationships that fans develop with *Mad Men*'s characters, their motivations for writing, and the parts of the show that interest them the most. In this chapter we'll explore how fans creatively engage with *Mad Men* through fan fiction.

#MadMen in 140 Characters or Less

According to fan studies scholar Francesca Coppa, fan fiction has a long history that goes back to fanzines from the 1930s. Today, a great deal of fan fiction is found online, most often in the form of full-length stories with beginnings, middles, and ends. But the popularity of social networking tools has led to the creation of new forms of fan fiction. And the form of *Mad Men* fan fiction that received the most attention appeared on Twitter.

Many *Mad Men* fans likely remember the controversy surrounding this pioneering use of Twitter's short messaging capabilities. As mentioned in chapter 1, during season two of the series, *Mad Men* characters including Don Draper, Peggy Olson, Joan Holloway, and Roger Sterling popped up on Twitter and started tweeting about their lives. While many people believed the Twitter versions of the characters were the product of a brilliant marketing strategy created by AMC, the tweeting *Mad Men* were actually fans role-playing as the characters. As media scholar Henry Jenkins explained in a 2009 post on his blog, "We can think of these tweets as fan fiction in its most spared down form — these tweets represented attempts to get inside the heads (or inhabit the bodies) of fictional characters and see . . . events from their perspective."

Just like story-length fan fic, Twitter let fans extend their experience with *Mad Men*. On the one hand, it was a little odd that a modern technology was being used to continue the story of a television show about the 1960s. On the other, Twitter offered a natural outlet for all the empathy and fascination fans feel for *Mad Men*'s characters. The tweeting fans were able to perform as their favorite characters, adopting those characters' points of view. Meanwhile other fans could pretend they were interacting with the real characters through Twitter. They could subscribe to the characters' updates, ask them questions, and get answers almost immediately. Also and importantly, the barrier to entry on Twitter was lower than with story-length fan fiction. The characters' tweets were quick to read and respond to, enabling fans to invest minimal time and effort while still being part of the fun.

The fans playing the Twitter *Mad Men* characters enhanced other fans' engagement and interest in the show. And the Twitter characters enabled both the tweeting fans and the fans reading their tweets to further immerse themselves in the world of *Mad Men*. This goes back to the idea of transportation we talked about in chapter 2. *Mad Men* on Twitter was another way for fans to transport themselves into the show's story and connect with its characters. Soon Don and the other characters gained thousands of followers.

Then their accounts were disabled. Twitter misinterpreted AMC's request to learn the identities of the individuals behind the accounts. Believing the television network had issued a copyright challenge, the social network suspended the offending accounts. The fan outcry against AMC because of the suspension and the eventual reinstatement of the user accounts has been thoroughly discussed elsewhere. The episode is far from forgotten though. It remains a cautionary tale for media industry professionals who wish to avoid alienating their fans because of overzealous protection of their intellectual property.

For us as media psychologists, the saga of the *Mad Men* characters of Twitter demonstrates fans' investment in the show and the innovative ways they found to leverage new technologies to sustain the story lines depicted in each episode. (Ginsberg, the copywriter whose extreme paranoia over the installation of Sterling Cooper & Partners' new computer leads him to cut off his own nipple, would be horrified—although, ironically for a man who hates computers, he currently has more than one Twitter account.)

In their 2013 book *Spreadable Media: Creating Value and Meaning in a Networked Culture*, Henry Jenkins, Sam Ford, and Joshua Green noted that the *Mad Men* characters on Twitter mostly stayed within the boundaries set by the show (something fans call "canon"—more on that later). While this is true for many fandoms that role-play on Twitter, some of them also occasion-

Figure 10. Michael Ginsberg currently has two separate Twitter accounts users can follow.

ally diverge from their source material and create new stories. For example, there are numerous Twitter accounts for the television show *Supernatural* that follow alternative story lines that have not appeared on the series itself.

Some surprising *Mad Men* figures have appeared on Twitter over the years, like the ad agency's copy machine (@Xerox914), Ida Blankenship's ghost (@Idas_ghost), and our personal favorite, Duck Phillips's poor abandoned dog Chauncey (@chauncey_dog—the account still exists but has been inactive since 2011). However, most of the characters didn't create new narrative threads or re-envision parts of the story. This, of course, is why so many people believed the Twitter characters were sanctioned by AMC.

In *Becoming a Mad Man*, Bud Caddell's 2009 report about his experiences as one of the tweeting *Mad Men*, he claimed it was devotion to the series that caused him and others to start tweeting as its characters in the first place. Caddell (who tweeted as @Bud_Melman, a Sterling Cooper mailroom worker—the account has been inactive since 2009) explained that it was simply a way for these fans to act out their fandom: "It was our appreciation of the subject matter, the writing, the acting, and the product as a whole that spurred our expression." Similarly, in a 2008 blog post, Paul Isakson, the fan who started the whole *Mad Men*-on-Twitter craze by tweeting as Don Draper (@don_draper—the account has not been active since 2010), said that he had no desire to "harm the character or the show in any way." These

 **chauncey_dog**
@chauncey_dog

I'm pretty sure if Don just adopted me he'd be more content. Who needs ladies or the hard stuff when you can have such a loyal companion.

Figure 11. A tweet by @chauncey_dog from October 7, 2010. The feed provides some (thankfully happy) resolution to Chauncey the Dog's story after his abandonment by Duck on the show.

fans didn't want to undermine the series Matthew Weiner and AMC were creating. They weren't interested in being compensated for their work, either. They simply wanted to stay in that world with those characters longer.

Yet, many of these tweeting fans also saw the incredible marketing potential in what they were creating. We noted in chapter 1 that Helen Klein Ross, who tweets as @BettyDraper, works in advertising. According to Caddell, she wasn't alone; a surprising number of the tweeting *Mad Men* were also in the advertising, marketing, and public-relations industries. This included Paul Isakson and Carri Bugbee, who tweeted as @PeggyOlson. Many advertising professionals are big *Mad Men* fans — something we will explore in further detail in chapter 8 — and the connections of the Mad Men on Twitter to advertising enabled them to see the ways they could use Twitter to extend *Mad Men*'s brand and further engage its audience. They were perplexed, then, that Matthew Weiner and AMC didn't share this vision and showed no interest in working with the fans behind the Twitter characters.

Caddell recounts that some of the tweeting Mad Men approached AMC and its ad agency about working with them to create more complex Twitter stories between *Mad Men* episodes. They were only met with consternation and ultimately silence. Similarly, in his 2012 book, *The Art of Immersion*, Frank Rose describes what happened when Helen Klein Ross met Matthew Weiner. Although Weiner said he enjoyed Ross's tweets as Betty, he was un-

Figure 12. A tweet by @bettydraper from April 13, 2014, the day of the premiere of the first half of season seven.

willing to tell her about upcoming Betty story lines she could use in her Twitter role-playing. So although they allowed the fans' activities to continue, *Mad Men*'s producers clearly preferred to draw a line between their intellectual property and the tweeting fans.

The producers' position ensured that only they had the power to truly further the show's story line. Yet Ross felt the producers missed an opportunity to expand *Mad Men* beyond its weekly time slot. After all, the *Mad Men* characters on Twitter were essentially marketing that the network didn't have to pay for. Harnessing its power could be to the show's advantage.

Paul Isakson even admitted that he started tweeting as Don as a kind of research project. Isakson wanted to see if he could extend a character from television into social media and as a result have people "connect to that character and the show in even more meaningful ways." In other words, Isakson wanted to see if fans would embrace the content they loved in new, nontraditional media.

The success of Isakson's experiment is noteworthy because, when he started tweeting in 2008, it brought *Mad Men*'s story to a burgeoning social network, demonstrating that people would follow their favorite stories wherever they went, including social media. In fact, film and television producers have been spreading details from their movies' and shows' stories across multiple media for years, including video games, web sites, blogs, comics, novels, and more — something called "transmedia storytelling," as described in chapter 1. Jenkins mentioned numerous examples of transmedia storytelling in a 2007 blog post, such as the animated show *The Clone Wars*, which bridged the gap between the first and second *Star Wars* prequel films, the web site for the television series *Dawson's Creek* that let fans read the main character's journal, and the films, animated series, comics, and video games that together told the story of *The Matrix*. More recent examples include the fictional TED talk that filled in the back story for the *Alien* prequel, *Prometheus*, the blog kept by *How I Met Your Mother* character Barney Stinson, and the social media accounts that enhance the web series *The Lizzie Bennet Diaries*.

Isakson and the other *Mad Men* characters on Twitter also blurred the lines between content producers and consumers. Although *Mad Men*'s producers did not accept the activity on Twitter as "official," the *Mad Men* tweeters did such a professional job playing the show's characters that other fans continued to follow and enjoy the additional *Mad Men* content they provided, despite the knowledge that it was fan-created. Of course, fans have always creatively extended and repurposed the stories they love in fan fiction, fan art, cosplay, and other forms. But the ability of fans to share their creative works online, and in this case through social media, has greatly increased their visibility and influenced both audiences' and producers' ideas about what entertainment content can be.

Many of the Mad Men on Twitter used the attention they received from the controversy surrounding their activities to enhance their professional standings. Both Carri Bugbee and Helen Klein Ross won Shorty Awards, which recognize the best social-media content creators, for their efforts. So while the saga of the tweeting Mad Men was reported as a David and Goliath story, digging into the incident presents something murkier and even more fascinating—something that could only happen in a world where fans can use the Internet to become and interact as the television characters they love.

In the end, the *Mad Men* fans on Twitter created new content as a means to both express their love of the show and to test the boundaries of the opportunities offered by new technology. However, considering the industry ties of these fans as well as the brief length of their tweets, it is hard to determine how much this short-form fan fiction reflects the average fans' thoughts about *Mad Men* itself. To get a more thorough picture of what fan fiction can tell us about how fans respond to the show, we now turn our attention to story-length fan fiction.

... The Long of It

We analyzed the text of every *Mad Men* fan-fiction story available as of September 2014 from the major fan-fiction archives, FanFiction.net and Archive of Our Own. The analysis enabled us to explore which elements of the show sparked *Mad Men* fan-fiction writers' imaginations, including which story lines they wanted to extend or change, which characters they wanted to spend more time with or imagine themselves as, and which relationships they cared about the most or would like to see happen.

These 337 pieces of fan fiction by 164 writers represented a wide range of content ratings and categories. The archives we gathered the stories from designate several ratings and categories that writers can assign to their fan fiction to inform readers about the kind of content they can expect if they choose to read a particular story. Ratings range from G, meaning appropriate for general audiences, to E, meaning explicit content. The majority of the fan fiction we analyzed was rated T, meaning it is appropriate for audiences 13 and older and was categorized as "het," meaning it featured heterosexual romances.

We also surveyed *Mad Men* fan-fiction readers and writers so they could tell us in their own words their reasons for choosing fan fiction as an outlet for their fandom. Common wisdom states that fan-fiction writers and readers are usually teenage girls. There's some evidence for this, too. A study by FFN Research showed that the average FanFiction.net user in 2010 was a 15.8-year-old girl. Meanwhile, a 2013 survey of Archive of Our Own by Lulu, to which more than 10,000 users responded, found most participants were female and had an average age of 25.1. These demographics are similar to those of our forty-two survey respondents, the vast majority of whom — 86 percent — were female. In addition, a third of our respondents fell between the ages of eighteen and twenty-four, but we also had respondents in every age bracket up to and including the 65-to-74-year-old range. The group was well educated, with 93 percent having attended at least some college and 61 percent holding a bachelor's degree or higher. Most of the respondents had been *Mad Men* fans since the beginning of the show and over 75 percent described their level of fandom as either medium or high. Finally, 62 percent of the respondents were both readers and writers of *Mad Men* fan fiction.

Our analysis of *Mad Men* fan fiction, along with the thoughtful responses of many of the survey participants, demonstrates how active and engaged these fans are. Their fan fiction used small details from the show as jumping off points for complete stories, explored the roads not taken by the show's writers and producers, and enabled them to give voice to the characters' inner lives. Their stories clearly allowed them to grapple with this nuanced series and its complicated characters.

Identifying with Peggy

Of the show's many characters we found that Peggy was by far the one who appeared most frequently in *Mad Men* fan-fiction stories. While Don Draper was the second-most-written-about character, he was not mentioned nearly as often as Peggy. This was somewhat surprising because, although Peggy is a major character, the show is ultimately centered on Don, and he is the character most associated with *Mad Men*. The focus on Peggy, then, indicates that many writers identify with her and want to spend time seeing the world through her eyes. Identification, as we discussed in chapter 2, is a bond with a character in which you merge with the character and start to see life from her point of view. When you identify with a character, you get inside her head and experience things as if you were that character.

Media psychologist Jonathan Cohen observed that fans are more likely to identify with characters they believe are similar to them in some way. This can be based on common demographics, but it can also be based on fans' ability to understand and empathize with what a character is going through. Given that Peggy is one of the most modern, progressive characters on *Mad Men*, as well as a character who experiences a great deal of change throughout the series, it makes sense that she would be a point of entry into that world for many fan-fiction writers.

Some survey respondents were attracted to Peggy because of her position as a career woman in a time that didn't always acknowledge her talents. One said that "[Peggy] is a strong, independent woman, yet there are many barriers and obstacles she faces." Another noted that Peggy had an "interesting perspective for a woman during that era." And another observed, "Peggy has the most character growth of anybody . . . over the run of the show. She's complicated and has a lot of self-doubt, insecurity and delusion—yet is a strong, positive woman who always pushes herself to achieve, despite the external and initial conflicts in her life. She's easy to root for without being saccharine."

Gender also likely plays an important role in *Mad Men* fan-fiction writers' and readers' ability to identify with Peggy. Fan-fiction writers typically write under pseudonyms and pen names, so we can't always know their genders for sure. But as we mentioned, fan fiction is usually a female endeavor. And given that 86 percent of our survey respondents were women, there is some evidence that *Mad Men* fan-fiction writers and readers are mostly female. These fans' common gender with Peggy likely enhances their identification with her and her struggles.

In support of this idea, we found that a majority of female survey respondents identified Peggy as the character they most enjoyed reading and writing about. One respondent explained that "I just really relate to this character. I understand her frustrations and heartbreak." Another said, "I identify with [Peggy] and want to see her in different scenarios." A third respondent declared, "I see parts of myself in her." And a fourth enjoyed putting herself in Peggy's shoes: "I like to explore the character, to try to view things [through] her eyes and kind of imagine what she thinks and feels about the things that happened to her, and about the people in her life."

In contrast, Peggy wasn't a favorite to read or write about for any of the six men who took our survey. In fact, all the men identified a male character as their favorite. Don Draper was mentioned most often, but both Pete Campbell and Stan Rizzo were also characters the male respondents enjoyed reading and writing fan fiction about.

Stories about Peggy often focus on her romantic life and her struggles as a working woman. For our survey respondents Peggy-centric stories were a way to explore the character's growth over the course of the show, to grapple with the discrimination and difficulties the character faces, and to negotiate the challenging relationships she experiences with the men in her life.

One respondent told us that Peggy is the character "I enjoy watching evolve on the show. However, I only read fan fiction about her when it also features my other favorite characters such as Stan Rizzo, Michael Ginsb[e]rg, or Don Draper." Another explained, "I like [Peggy's] personality, she's a strong character who's very well developed and there's issues about her past or other things that the show [doesn't] touch, so it's interesting to see these things in fan fiction." Another prefers fan fiction that gives the woman a chance to transcend her circumstances: "I like reading things where Peggy is able to overcome the gender discrimination she can't escape in the show. Peggy would be a modern day hero, but she's set in the sixties where she is unfortunately a tragic hero due to the time period. Fan fiction helps her break those chains." And another respondent claimed, "Peggy is the character with the most dynamic arc. I appreciate that she's not only grown over seven seasons, but also regressed. She's also [a] parallel of Don, but without his toxicity. Plus, she's female and she's fascinating."

Fan-fiction stories about Peggy often use the advertising offices of Sterling Cooper and the other agencies the character works at on *Mad Men*, as well as the specific advertising campaigns she works on, as their backdrop. Not only do these stories give the reader a feeling for the intricacies of her professional life, but they also put her in close proximity to the other *Mad Men* characters that shape her world.

In particular, because many of Peggy's relationships are with people she knows through work, the advertising agencies make the perfect setting for her to encounter the people and scenarios that drive the fan fiction featuring her character. For example, LSquared80's story "Other Ways of Speaking" features a series of flirtations between Peggy and Stan at the offices of Sterling Cooper & Partners. In this story the workplace offers a means for exploring the characters' feelings about one another and where their relationship might go.

In fact, many fan-fiction writers used the advertising agency and the ad campaigns that occupy the characters' time at the office to establish their stories in the familiar world of *Mad Men*. But as with fan fiction about Peggy, in many cases the goings-on at the office function as the background for stories that delve into the characters' personal relationships and inner struggles. We'll talk more about Peggy and her relationships in a bit.

Don and Motivations for Writing

While not as prevalent as Peggy stories, there was still plenty of Don-centric fan fiction in our analysis. Don stories often examined his life at home and especially his relationships with his second and third wives, Betty and Megan, and his daughter Sally. Fan fiction featuring Don illustrates two reasons audiences enjoy and appreciate narrative fiction.

On the one hand, just as on the show, Don often appeared in stories in which he engages in activities of a more . . . let's say mature nature. Some of these stories are pretty graphic in their descriptions of Don's sexual exploits. For example, the stories "Need You" by Quills2 and "Empowerment" by Rinat114 feature intense sexual encounters between a post-divorce Don and Betty. These explicit stories use the characters' desire for sex with each other as a means to get them back together, however briefly.

Writers create fan fiction that focuses on detailed sex scenes because of what media psychologists label "hedonic motivation." These stories come from the fan-fiction writers' desire to create stories that are pleasurable and entertaining—both for themselves and their readers. The sexually explicit content that these stories feature is emotionally satisfying to the women who write and read them. Rinat114's "Empowerment" is written from Betty's perspective, easily enabling the writer to explore the character's reasons for deciding to have a sexual liaison with Don after their split. And Quills2's "Need You" explores how Don's sexual interest in Betty arises from his need for her presence in the face of his uncertainty about his marriage to Megan. In these stories it is Betty who has the power in the relationship—and she uses it to get what she wants from Don sexually.

Some of our survey respondents' reasons for reading and writing *Mad Men* fan fiction acknowledge the pleasure they get from it. One simply explained that reading *Mad Men* fan fiction "is fun." Another said she read and wrote *Mad Men* fan fiction "to resolve all the (sexual) tension on the show and in my pants." Of course, this reaction to fan fiction is common in many fandoms. Numerous scholars have speculated about the reasons fan fiction is appealing to women. One conclusion, articulated by fan-culture columnist Elizabeth Minkel in a 2014 *New Statesman* article, is that in a world in which the majority of what we see onscreen is driven by the male perspective, fan fiction offers women and other marginalized groups the chance to express themselves, their interests, and their desires in ways that aren't addressed by mainstream media. So writing and reading sexually explicit fan fiction gives women a chance to experience stories that speak to their pleasures and preferences and charisma are.

On the other hand, many fan-fiction writers used their stories to examine the reasons behind Don's frequent infidelities, the lies he told about his past as Dick Whitman, and the fallout that occurred when this secret was revealed. In the story "The End of Camelot," for example, writer Scarlett88 explores Betty's perspective as she learns the truth about Don's past: "[Betty's] world came to a halt when she finally discovered what Don had kept in his locked desk—a whole past life, a life that she was not privy to nor a part of. The truth of the matter was she knew nothing about the man that she married. He treasured his secrets, and he preferred keeping her in the dark because it was more convenient for him."

In these instances the stories are written as a means for making sense of various elements of *Mad Men*, including the emotions, motivations, and thoughts the characters don't express on the show. These pieces of fan fiction are written out of what media psychologists label "eudaimonic motivation." They reveal fan-fiction writers' desire to get at the show's deeper meanings and truths. Of course, the deeper truths that fans glean from the show are highly personal. So each individual fan-fiction writer and reader may be interested in exploring different parts of the show based on the story elements that are most meaningful to her.

Many survey respondents appeared to be seeking this kind of meaning from *Mad Men* fan fiction. For example, one explained that she read fan fiction because "the show doesn't explore certain character arcs or relationships that I'm more interested in." Another respondent concurred, saying she read fan fiction because "I'm interested in seeing other people's perspectives on the characters, particularly the viewpoints and relationships between the women because those are the most interesting parts of the show to me." Meanwhile, a respondent said she wrote *Mad Men* fan fiction "to explore how characters could change and grow. To better understand the characters."

Another agreed, stating that writing *Mad Men* fan fiction enabled her to "flesh out ideas about my favorite characters."

Canon vs. Fanon

Different kinds of motivation are one way to understand why people read and write *Mad Men* fan fiction (and why audiences watch the show too), but scholars have studied fan fiction from many other perspectives. In some cases scholars have emphasized the fact that fan fiction must work within the boundaries set by the television show or other source material on which the fic is based. The source material, called canon, sets the parameters for the world of many fan-fiction stories, including the setting, characters, and plotlines.

Of course, as we saw above in AMC's reaction to the fans who role-play as *Mad Men* characters on Twitter, producers like to distinguish clearly between the official content they produce and any work their content inspires fans to create. And the producers have the ability and incentives to keep those boundaries firm, because as the originators of the content they have economic incentives and copyright laws on their side. But fans feel an emotional attachment to the entertainment they love, and that attachment moves them to spend time thinking about, scrutinizing, and analyzing the source material.

Fan fiction and other fan works help fans make sense of their feelings about the plot points and character arcs depicted in the canon content, regardless of the fact that they aren't the official "owners" of that content. As one survey respondent explained, "Sometimes I obsess a little [during] . . . the current [*Mad Men*] season and [writing fan fiction] helps me get thoughts out of my head." As researchers Louisa Stein and Kristina Busse have pointed out, the source material sets the limitations for fans as they interpret and transform various elements of canon in ways that feel meaningful and satisfying to them.

In the *Mad Men* fan fiction we analyzed, many stories that explored canon sought to fill in gaps in the plotlines, take stock of the characters' emotional or psychological states, or examine the characters' relationships with one another. For example, Peggy's romantic entanglements on *Mad Men* were often the basis for stories that delve into her relationships with Pete Campbell and Ted Chaough. While neither of these relationships (or "ships" in fan circles) were successful on the show, fan-fiction stories often reimagined a happy ending for these couples, especially for the Peggy/Ted relationship.

On the show, of course, Ted promises Peggy he will leave his wife for her but instead leaves her (and New York) to move with his family to California. Many fan-fiction stories explored the emotional fallout from Ted's choice, while others worked to maneuver the characters back together despite the obstacles set up by the series. The stories that envisioned Peggy and Ted eventually coupling up operate as a form of wish fulfillment, depicting a more positive outcome for a relationship that abruptly went sour on the show. On *Mad Men* Peggy never has the opportunity to process her feelings or fight for the relationship because Ted's departure is so unexpected. Writing fan-fiction stories that finally get the characters together, as explained in chapter 2, is a way for fans who wanted Peggy to get her happy ending with Ted to resolve what was left unresolved on the show. Of reading fan fiction about this relationship, one of our survey respondents claimed, "I think it is interesting to see . . . where their relationship might lead despite the obvious problems they have that drove them apart."

Some fan-fiction writers also wrote about the Peggy/Ted relationship because they wished to explore their conflicted feelings about it. In order for Peggy and Ted to be together, Ted must leave his family, a plot development with moral ramifications that made many fans uncomfortable. However, as we noted earlier, many fan-fiction writers and readers identify with Peggy. As a result, they view her positively and want good things for her. When the character connects with Ted on the show, these fans root for the relationship to work out for her sake. But if she gets the relationship she wants, Peggy also plays a role in destroying a marriage, a moral lapse that crosses the line for some. So these fans feel internally conflicted — they want Peggy to be happy, but they also want to maintain their positive perception of her. Fan fiction enables fans to explore the moral and emotional implications of this conflict. As one survey respondent confided, "Even though I am happily married and I abhor the idea of cheating, I just really like the two of these characters together."

Fan fic that tackled the Peggy/Pete relationship was often less optimistic about the prospects for that pairing. A number of pieces explored the relationship within the context of the aftermath of Peggy's decision to give up their child for adoption. As fans will remember, while Pete eventually found out about the child, the show left this story line open-ended. The audience remained in the dark about where their child had ultimately ended up and how both Peggy and Pete felt about what happened. As one survey respondent summed it up, "Their relationship is unfinished. [On the show] they have both moved on and become different people, but their underlying connection is completely ignored. These two people had a baby together — I want resolution!" Much like the fan fiction that re-envisioned a more satisfying resolution for the Peggy/Ted pairing, many fan-fiction stories also sought to flesh out a resolution for the Peggy/Pete relationship.

Similarly, many fan-fiction stories explored Don's relationships with his family, and in particular with his wife Betty. These stories often focused on the difficulties Betty and Don faced in their marriage and the reasons for their eventual split. Fan-fiction writers tackled the couple's issues from a variety of different angles in order to explore the characters' internal emotional reactions and the things their characters didn't give voice to on the show.

One survey respondent explained that fan fiction featuring the Betty/ Don relationship was appealing because it comes directly from the series, observing that "I find this 'ship' integral to the series. . . . They have so much history together, some of which has been touched on, but much has been unmentioned. I love reading different interpretations of this couple, what could have been, what should have been, etc. There is so much untapped drama found with this couple, they have three children together, they cannot escape each other, no matter how hard they try." So fan fiction about the Peggy/Ted, Peggy/Pete, and Don/Betty relationships often uses the events from the show as a jumping-off point. Fan writers then create new plotlines and imagine new interactions between the characters that take the story in directions fans find more fulfilling.

In contrast, many fan-fiction writers go outside of canon to explore alternative plotlines, relationships, and settings for the characters. When these fan-created alterations to the source material become established in a fan community and come up again and again in fan-fiction stories, they're considered fanon. In the introduction to their 2006 book, *Fan Fiction and Fan Communities in the Age of the Internet*, Kristina Busse and Karen Hellekson note that fanon is especially potent when an alternative understanding of a character or plot point becomes established in the fan community in spite of canon's lack of support for it. Fanon stories tend to exemplify the proposal of some scholars that fan fiction is a transgressive practice. They are the clearest examples of fan-fiction writers appropriating the official source material and reworking it to make it their own—a process Jenkins famously referred to in his 1992 book as "textual poaching."

Several examples of fanon appeared in the *Mad Men* fan fiction we analyzed. Most were romantic pairings—in particular, the romantic pairings of Peggy and Stan as well as Peggy and Don were popular revisions of the characters' platonic relationships from the majority of the series. These relationships were especially popular with our survey respondents, who were reading and writing fan fic before the second half of season seven aired. Many explained that stories featuring these couples enabled them to get from fan fiction what the show was not providing for them. One respondent noted, "Stan and Peggy have a lot of depth because he 'gets' her work persona plus there is a sexual tension that exists in their relationship." Of her interest in a Peggy/Don relationship, another said, "I honestly don't believe they will ever form a romantic relationship in the actual show. It's nice to have that 'what-if' moment."

So fan fiction offers the opportunity to experience pairings the show's canon does not. In these cases fan fiction enables fans who are dissatisfied with the relationships portrayed on the show to remix them in ways they may ultimately find more satisfying. The desire to see these relationships become part of the story inspires fans' creativity. Canon doesn't provide the romance these fans are looking for, so they take matters into their own hands by writing their own version of the story or seeking out fan fiction that fulfills their wish to see a particular relationship happen.

Slash fan fiction, in which two same sex characters who are heterosexual in the source material are romantically paired in fan-fiction stories, is especially representative of fanon. In our analysis a number of examples of slash fan fiction appeared. In fact, almost 20 percent of the stories we analyzed were slash stories. A majority involved male/male pairings like Don and Roger or Don and Pete, but there were also several that included female/female pairings like Peggy and Joan. Such stories place the characters in romantic situations that are highly unlikely to be featured on the show. What's more, slash stories also let fans challenge the constraints of the traditional 1960s gender roles and rampant heterosexism depicted on *Mad Men*.

For example, in MeredithDraper's story "Overdoing It," Don initiates a sexual encounter with an uncertain Pete after the pair is forced to share a hotel room. To Pete's surprise and confusion he enjoys the experience. And in Day Man's story "The Plan," Roger plans to get Don drunk in order to have sex with him. But after calling Don into his office, Don turns the tables and has his way with Roger on Roger's desk.

Busse and Hellekson have observed that slash stories are often based on fans' perception of a homoerotic subtext in the source material. It could be argued that *Mad Men* hints at certain slash couplings because of the characters' relationships at work. Regardless of orientation, however, the show suggests many of the noncanon romances discussed here. Whether a writer pairs Peggy and Don or Peggy and Joan, the close working relationships of these characters on *Mad Men* often serve as the starting point for evolving a platonic relationship into a romantic one.

In many cases, then, even when fan-fiction writers are re-envisioning the relationships on *Mad Men* to create new couplings, they still take cues from the show itself. This demonstrates how blurry the boundaries of canon can be. Fans interpret things differently and one fan's understanding of canon may be different from another's. Regardless, one survey respondent summed up perhaps the most important thing about the *Mad Men* fan-fiction relationships from outside canon when she told us, "It's hot."

Exploring Characters

Whether the couples in the *Mad Men* fan fiction we analyzed were canon or fanon, one common feature was that the writers and their readers wanted to spend more time with the characters. One reason fans have this desire is because they form what media psychologists call "parasocial relationships" with the *Mad Men* characters. A parasocial relationship is a lot like a social relationship with a real-life friend or family member. Just as in real life, you have to meet and spend time with a person before you can form a meaningful relationship with her. In the case of a character on a television show, this means watching her show and paying attention to the character. This is called "parasocial interaction," a concept originated by Donald Horton and Richard Wohl in 1956.

When you're watching *Mad Men* have you ever found yourself reacting to a character's behavior as if it was really happening? Maybe you've even shouted at the television or rolled your eyes at a character's flawed behavior. These are examples of parasocial interactions, which are different from identifying with a character. When you identify with a character, you see the world from that character's perspective, like the survey respondents we discussed earlier who wrote stories from Peggy's point of view. In contrast, when you interact parasocially, you maintain your own perspective and are aware that the character you're interacting with has a perspective that's different from yours.

So parasocial interaction is like any other social interaction, just one-sided. You form a parasocial relationship after you've spent enough time with a character to start thinking about him outside of the times you're watching him. Once you've formed such a relationship, you can enhance it through activities like discussing the character with friends or writing and reading about the character, sometimes in the form of fan fiction.

Reading and writing *Mad Men* fan fiction is an opportunity for fans to engage in the parasocial bonds they have built with different characters from the show. This is especially true of fan-fiction stories featuring secondary characters who don't get a lot of screen time, such as Ted and Stan. Stories that give these characters starring roles let fan-fiction writers and readers spend more time with them than the show provides. Through fan fiction, fans can explore the aspects of these characters they enjoy the most outside the constraints imposed by the source material.

Many of our survey respondents implied that writing and reading *Mad*

Men fan fiction enabled them to further develop their parasocial connections with the characters. For instance, one said, "All the characters I think about writing about in the *Mad Men* fandom are ones I'm curious as to how their head and their heart work." Parasocial relationships cause fans to ponder characters in an effort to better understand them, just as you might attempt to comprehend the actions of your friends or family members in real life.

The ability of fans to form parasocial relationships with the characters of their favorite popular media demonstrates one way in which they conceptualize and relate to characters as if they were real people. This is not to say that fans don't understand that television and movie characters are not real. But real or not, our natural social instincts kick in when we're confronted with another person. So the *Mad Men* characters offer social information to their fans that may be just as potent as the social information offered by the real people in our lives.

For example, one survey respondent devoted time to analyzing the character Betty in hopes of understanding her better: "The fact that I find this character underdeveloped on the series makes it fun and exciting to write for her, I am creating little snippets or factoids about her that were never mentioned on the series (but maybe implied). I find the character layered, trapped in a role of motherhood when she is still confused as to who she is. There is so much inner-turmoil for this character. . . . I find her a sympathetic character, even when she is at her very worst (lashing out at her children or others). She is someone who wants to be a good wife and mother, wants to love those around her, but she is extremely guarded and cannot seem to love herself."

It's possible that sometimes *Mad Men*'s fictional characters can seem even more relevant to us than the people we know in real life because we see so much more of the characters' lives than we do of the lives of our real-life acquaintances. By considering what *Mad Men* characters have done or might do, we can vicariously experience new things or learn new information we might not have access to otherwise. This is supported by this observation from one of the survey respondents, "Writing Betty lets me explore my own suburban white housewife angst through the lens of history. It also lets me imagine a better, more powerful, future for her as she, like many of her generation, discovers women's liberation." This individual is comparing her experiences to Betty's while also envisioning a more empowered future for the character — a future that may resemble her hopes for herself.

Similarly, of her love of Peggy, another respondent said, "I can identify with her challenges as a professional woman, and I get to live vicariously a bit through the plots and characterization in the [fan fiction] stories. This isn't true for all works — this is a fandom where I like to see positive outcomes rather than high drama situations." Fan fiction enables this respondent to experience positive resolutions for Peggy's struggles in the working world. She may also use fan fiction to vicariously experiment with ways to resolve the professional hurdles she encounters in her own life. Narrative fiction can be a potent point of reference in people's lives. And fan fiction, in particular, gives fans the opportunity to transform their favorite stories and characters in ways that are more personally relevant than the source material alone.

Writing the Past from the Present

Interestingly, although the *Mad Men* fan-fiction writers in our analysis chose to write stories about a television show whose time period is a major attraction for viewers, the writers often didn't emphasize period details in their fan fiction. This is not to imply that *Mad Men* fan fiction completely ignores the show's 1960s setting. Some writers incorporated rich period details into their stories.

For instance, in "The Gay Love Child of Dick Whitman" (a very non-sixties title, indeed), justincbenedict reminds the reader of the story's period setting by referencing historical information. In one chapter of the story, Harry Crane discusses ad placement for the television show *Ironside*, which first aired in 1967. The character also interacts with Sirhan Sirhan, who assassinated Robert Kennedy in 1968 — an event referenced during a season six episode of *Mad Men*. For those familiar with them, the experience of reading this story is enhanced by these historical details.

A few survey respondents felt that part of the appeal of writing fan fiction for *Mad Men* is the show's time period. One noted that she wrote *Mad Men* fan fiction because she finds "the characters and the era fascinating." Another writer commented, "This show is fun to write for because it gives me an excuse to research fun and obscure areas of recent American cultural history, which is similar to the appeal of watching the show."

Often, though, many writers chose not to address the show's period setting directly, making it hard to determine whether their stories should be seen as commentaries on the 1960s or simply as explorations of concerns the writers have about the present day. In the story "Hiding in Plain Sight," for example, wildcard47 reflects on Peggy's ascension at Sterling Cooper and her struggles as a woman in a workplace dominated by men. Despite its references to Sterling Cooper and the steno pool, the story could be understood as a description of the feelings of a woman in a sexist work environment today.

In a 2012 study of online fan conversations about weddings on *Mad Men*, Lynne M. Webb, Marceline Thompson Hayes, Hao-Chieh Chang, and Marcia M. Smith found that the fans' critiques were often based on the values of the present day, as opposed to those of the show's time period. And, as we've discussed in other chapters, our research revealed that fans often compare the 1960s depicted on *Mad Men* to the present day. Fan fiction that comments on the restrictions and constraints of the sixties, even in indirect and subtle ways, provides further evidence that fans often think about the show's time period from the perspective of today. Their stories may delve into the way the characters feel about their experiences in the sixties, but the fan-fiction writers' point of view is understandably locked in the early twenty-first century. Since *Mad Men* is often considered a commentary on the present day, it's not surprising that there are many examples of *Mad Men* fan fiction that fall into this category.

Performing New Episodes

Regardless of whether writers directly address the sixties or not, *Mad Men* fan fiction is automatically tied to the show's time period simply because readers' knowledge of the series makes it that way. By evoking Don Draper's smoking and drinking, for example, fan-fiction stories reference the character's habits from the show. In the process, the stories also subtly reference the show's time period. After all, modern-day executives rarely smoke or drink quite so much — especially at the office. So *Mad Men* fan-fiction writers use the knowledge readers have of the show to their advantage.

The stories in our analysis often referred to the physical features of both the advertising agency's offices and the characters themselves. These things engage readers' imaginations, enabling fan-fiction writers to essentially produce new *Mad Men* episodes in their readers' minds. Coppa has claimed that fan fiction is more like a theatrical performance than literature, and many of the *Mad Men* fan-fiction stories we analyzed supported that observation. Much like a theatrical company performs a famous play as a way to provide a different take on the material, these stories evoke the characters and settings that fans are familiar with but alter them to fit the writer's vision. This is how writers enable readers to imagine their stories being performed by the cast of *Mad Men*.

To some degree this could also be said of the *Mad Men* characters on Twitter, discussed at the beginning of the chapter. On his blog in 2009, Jenkins asserted that while story-length fan fiction may be a performance, Twitter fan fiction could be considered "a kind of performance art" due to its shortened form. Either way, *Mad Men* fan fiction lets writers share their perspectives on the show and lets readers discover how others understand it. This adds to the richness of the *Mad Men* fandom experience.

As noted, television show characters can be a source of social information. And viewing and evaluating characters that are meaningful to us can help us decide how to feel about and react to situations in our own lives. At the same time, fan communities offer their own interpretations of characters and plotlines from their favorite television shows, providing another source of social information to individual fans. Writing and reading fan fiction is one creative way for fans to connect and bond over their different interpretations of a show's plotlines and the various parasocial relationships they have formed with its characters.

Learning how other fans understand a show can be especially valuable social information, particularly for fans of a layered and nuanced show like *Mad Men*. While the producers of some shows pay more attention to fan sentiment than others, fans generally can't talk to them or influence the course of the series directly. So fan communities offer the next best thing. Fan communities are open, interactive, and collaborative. In fan communities, including fan-fiction communities, fans can make sense of their favorite series together by comparing notes and discussing their thoughts about what they've watched.

In fact, learning how other fans interpret the show was among the most popular reasons survey respondents provided for reading *Mad Men* fan fiction, and sharing one's perspectives about the show was among the most popular reasons for writing it. For example, one fan-fiction reader noted, "I like to see how other people interpret the characters, their personalities, and how they would react in different situations." And another observed, "When reading fiction, you get insight from other authors, other points of view that give you thoughts to ponder or inspiration to write for yourself." Meanwhile, a writer explained that she likes "to give others an opportunity to further explore the world of *Mad Men* through my eyes and thoughts." In these instances, fans turned to each other for information about how to comprehend *Mad Men*. The fan community helped individual fans deepen their understanding of the show, its plotlines, and its characters.

An Active Audience

Mad Men fans who read and write fan fiction are active audience members who are well informed about the show they love. Reading and writing fan fiction is one way these fans invest time in their fandom. This is both because reading and writing fan fiction is fun and because it gives them more opportunities to make sense of what they see on screen. After all, *Mad Men* is not known for its lengthy seasons. This leaves long hiatuses in which fans have no new "official" content. Several of the fan-fiction writers and readers we surveyed believed that fan fiction offered a worthwhile way to spend more time in the world they loved between *Mad Men* seasons. As one noted, fan fiction "satisfies my craving when no new canon content is available."

Fan fiction is often dismissed as derivative, amateur, or unnecessary for a well-written show like *Mad Men*. But as this chapter shows, what fans get out of fan fiction depends on what they are looking for from it. For many of the fan-fiction readers and writers we surveyed, fan fiction extended and enhanced their active engagement with the show and enabled them to share that engagement with other like-minded fans. These fans read and write fan fiction to puzzle out various aspects of a complex television show, to visit with their favorite characters, and to correct unsatisfying plotlines.

In the process *Mad Men* fans expand their understanding of and appreciation for the show. Fan fiction, whether in the form of a 140-character tweet or a longer story, lets *Mad Men* fan writers increase the meaning and resonance the show has for them — and for their readers. Fan-fiction writers "talk back" to the show by revisiting, revising, and re-envisioning various elements in their fan fiction. Now with the show ending after seven seasons, perhaps even more fans will seek out fan fiction as a way to continue their fandom of the series. For those who are interested, the Twitter usernames and fan-fiction stories mentioned throughout this chapter are a good place to start.

CHAPTER FIVE

The "Girls" of Mad Men

As we've mentioned, we spent an entire year doing research with the end goal of revealing the voices of *Mad Men* fans and helping unearth what the show meant to them. Fans don't speak with only one voice, so we worked to reveal common themes—how various groups saw the stories and characters. But in our conversations with each other and our analysis of the experiences of fans, something unexpected began to occur to us. We realized that there was another set of voices that we could bring to light—the voices of those who decided *not* to become fans. We discovered that unearthing that experience would be as valuable as revealing what those who did buy into the show thought and felt.

This actually started out as a personal story. One of us has a grown daughter who had declared her revulsion toward the show. Now, as media psychologists, we do understand that once we call ourselves fans, the show becomes part of our identity. Fritz Heider, a famous name from the early history of social psychology, formulated something called "balance theory." In a nutshell, Heider said that if I like you and you like Mary, then you will be upset if I don't like Mary, and I may become upset too. When it comes to fandom, if I like *Mad Men* and I like you, I want you to like *Mad Men* too. If you don't, I might wonder if you really like *me*! Everything is out of balance.

You may recall from your own experience that when *Mad Men* first aired, some of the press it got was focused on the shock value of the way women were treated on the show. This was blatant sexism, right? The show seemed to be a symbol of a kind of caveman mentality that had thankfully disappeared long ago. Or had it? These are some of the ideas we've discussed in the chapter called "That Was Then, This Is Now." We bring it up again here to look at this experience from another angle. We have focused on the people who embraced the show. What about those who rejected it, such as the adult daughter we mentioned. Why did she reject it? As psychologists, we, of course, have a theory: We think some people saw the depiction of sexism in the sixties as an indictment of that sexism, while others were turned off because they felt that the treatment was more of a celebration, or at least a tolerance, of that sexism and therefore something they couldn't bear to watch.

From our database of comments on *Mad Men* fan forums comes this post, from someone who obviously felt that way:

> What is wrong w/ me that I don't like *Mad Men*? I tried Netflixing the first season, but I found it incredibly depressing from the first scene onward—[another poster] was right, this show IS partly about White Male Privilege, and we're [men] never gonna have it that good again. So THAT depresses me already. Then there's the whole sad drinking thing, and. . . . Look, what is wrong w/ me that I don't like this show?

It's worth pausing here to mention that this comment belongs in the debate about whether it is cool or uncool to be a fan. People have sometimes used fan status as a good reason for social ostracism, but this commenter seems to be saying that if you are not a fan of a show that is currently popular, then that may be a reason for ostracism. Which is it: fan=reject or nonfan=reject? We think the answer is not only "both," but everything in between. In other words, fandom isn't a one-size-fits-all experience.

Some franchises don't seem to fully develop a critical mass that merits the word "fandom." Others seem to be the "fandom du jour": like the groovy sixties styles *Mad Men* dazzles us with, what's *hot* one moment can be *not* the next. Some fandoms feel low key (NPR?), some can feel timeless (Hitchcock?). And, of course, each fan brings a personality and an intensity to the way he engages with a franchise.

Getting back to the topic of multiple interpretations of a show, we mentioned earlier that one of the biggest fandoms in America rose up around Stephen Colbert—a gifted comic actor who played a character designed to be a parody of conservative pundit Bill O'Reilly. An interesting phenomenon behind Colbert's fandom is that the show attracted both liberals and conservatives. And the data indicate that many of the conservative fans were not aware that Colbert's O'Reilly-inspired character was intended to mock their perspective.

Mad Men's intent, we think, is a little less transparent than Colbert's. Did the show's creators wish to celebrate sexism (or, for that matter, racism and materialism) or did they intend to use fiction to shine a light on sexism? We interpret their vision as more consistent with the latter interpretation, but it is a point that can be easily debated.

This raises another hotly debated question in the study of the psychology of fandom: who decides on the intent of the show? Furthermore, is there only one canonical interpretation, even when it comes to intent? We say that both fans and show creators can contribute to these conversations about interpreting the text.

Finally, we would be remiss to miss another important point that this non-fan's comment raises about fandom: Notice that its author is questioning what his own problem is because he does not like *Mad Men*. Anecdotally, we have noticed that in today's media landscape, the pressure to be a fan of the most popular shows can be high. If *Game of Thrones* or *Breaking Bad* is hot right now, then you can't admit that you don't really care for either of them. We've talked about fandom as a marginalized identity. To this conversation we now add that not being a fan can be a marginalized identity today. In certain quarters being a fan of the hot ticket item is de rigueur, and those who are mocked are not the fans, but the nonfans.

Be that as it may, we now return to the main topic of this chapter—the representation of women and women's roles in *Mad Men*. As we noted, some viewers found that representation so repulsive that they could not bear to watch it. Those who did become fans struggled to make sense of how each of the key females of *Mad Men* navigated the social world as she experienced it.

Peggy, Betty, Joan, and Megan, and Yes, Sally: The "Girls" of *Mad Men*

In *Mad Men* women trying to make it in advertising face sexism and sexual harassment on a regular basis, as when Peggy was criticized for showing too little skin or when Bert refers to her as a "little girl" even after she has been a copywriter for some time. As wives and mothers the show's characters find themselves frustrated and unhappy. Naturally, we wanted to know what fans made of these gendered story lines.

Over the year that we researched the show, we analyzed fan commentary in online forums covering the life of the show through the first half of the seventh and final season. Drawing on a pool of some 800 comments on the topics of motherhood, office politics, and character identity, we examine what fans say about the women of *Mad Men* and, more specifically, what instances of gender politics and sexism fans care about most.

So what *do* fans say about the women of *Mad Men*? Fans find Betty as a great outlet for wish fulfillment of their baddest desires. Peggy is the woman whom fans are most likely to imagine themselves as. Megan is on the receiving end of a lot of fan criticism, yet some fans find resonance and meaning in her story line. Joan is condemned by some for using sex to achieve a position of power, while other fans are much more concerned with what she will do with it than how she achieved it. Fans have a great deal of emotional investment in Sally and are especially concerned with what will become of her at the close of the series. But first, we have to start at the beginning, with fan responses to how it all began.

Many fans said that when they first began watching *Mad Men*, it was a struggle for them to enjoy it because of the intense sexism experienced by the female characters. Viewers like our nonfan above even refused to continue watching the show because the level of sexism was too painful, too much of a reminder of how things once were. Looking back at the first episode, it is clear why the show was difficult for many to watch (more on that in a minute). For those of us able to stick with the show despite the initial shock of its portrayal of extreme chauvinism, a bigger picture became apparent, one in which changing gender roles and growing opportunities for women and the counterculture movement began to challenge sexism. One fan explains the importance of being open to these gradually emerging themes while watching:

You can't watch this show with the hindsight [that] science and research has provided for you in the nearly fifty years since these fictional accounts occurred. You have to be prescient to the fact that we know a lot more now, as a result of the women's liberation movement about what is better for our bodies and our children, why it's crucial that we continue to carry on and fight.

While there is an overall story arc across the seasons of *Mad Men* and it most certainly contains messages about gender roles, we are also invested in the stories of individual characters. These individual stories that we get wrapped up in allow us to experience that sting of gender injustices as well as the shifts. In this chapter we look at the individual character arcs of popular female characters and the aspects of these stories that viewers are most concerned with discussing, including the aspects of sexism and gender politics from the perspectives of our research on *Mad Men* fans.

Peggy Olson

The first glimpse we get of the office climate at Sterling Cooper Advertising is Peggy Olson riding up in the elevator with mid-level employees Ken Cosgrove, Paul Kinsey, and Harry Crane. They engage in sexually suggestive commentary directed at Peggy—with Ken asking the elevator operator to "take the long way" to their floor because he was "enjoying the view" of Peggy's backside. The theme of Peggy as sex object is heavily emphasized in this first episode. After getting off the elevator, Ken says, "She'll know what she's in for. Besides, you have to let them know what kind of guy you are. Then they'll know what kind of girl to be." To learn more about those first scenes that were so difficult for so many viewers we take a closer look at fans' reflections.

So what kind of girl did Peggy learn that she should be from this experience? One fan describes Peggy as a fast learner because at the end of her first day, she makes a move on her boss Don Draper—laying her hand on top of his and thanking him after he stands up to Pete for harassing her: "I think the fact that Don turns Peggy down is the point of that little scene. She already is learning that it is her work that will distinguish her and that Don, for all his philandering ways, respects her and gives her a chance (well, Teddy Rumson is the first to notice her talent, but Don goes with it and doesn't squelch her.)"

Don rejects Peggy's hint of openness, telling her instead, "I'm your boss,

Figure 13. The introductory scene to *Mad Men*'s fictional advertising firm, Sterling Cooper, is a young secretary by the name of Peggy Olson arriving for her first day of work (screen capture from season one, episode one, "Smoke Gets in Your Eyes").

not your boyfriend," then kindly says when she becomes embarrassed that they will start fresh in the morning. The mixed messages Peggy receives on her first day are polar opposites. Don emphasizes the importance that she commit to her job, while Pete, Ken, Joan, and even the switchboard "girls" re-iterate the importance of sex appeal. Peggy's lesson on sexual availability does not end once she heads home at the end of her first day. Pete Campbell — after mercilessly harassing Peggy for her appearance earlier that day — shows up that evening at Peggy's door after his bachelor party.

Viewers take differing stances regarding this event. Some believe that Peggy is in love with Pete (after knowing and being bullied by him for just one day). Others believe that Peggy is naive and excited that someone who is comparatively rich and successful like Pete is interested in her. Based upon the workplace orientation she received, this fan posits that Peggy may believe she needs to be sexually open in order to succeed.

You're forgetting that it was Pete who showed up at her door, drunk and horny. In our world of 2014, I can totally see a woman having the thought that it would be completely uncool to have sex with him, but this is 1960 and she is probably a virgin, or near to it. It's her first job straight out of secretarial school. . . . Peggy is from the lower middle class — it had to be dazzling to work in a Madison Avenue ad agency in 1960 when you came from an outer borough like Peggy.

Whichever point of view you endorse, Peggy's first day — and the show's first episode — vividly captures the intense sexism that women workers faced in the 1960s. It's not hard to understand why some people couldn't stand to watch.

Aside from Don, Peggy is the character we see the most across the first two episodes and throughout much of the series. As you read in chapter 4, many fan-fiction writers identify with Peggy because they can relate to both her gender and career. From our research, fans see Peggy as a trailblazer, not just within the advertising industry but for women of the 1960s in general. As the decade advances on *Mad Men*, fans watch Peggy battle both overt and implicit sexism from her superiors and coworkers alike. So what is it about the character of Peggy and her experiences that so many fans identify with? Recall from chapter 2 that the three components of identification are empathizing with the character, imagining oneself as the character, and merging with or thinking that you have become the character in some manner. Fans identify with Peggy in each of these ways.

In the fan-revered episode "The Suitcase," fans expressed empathy for Peggy when she is not invited to attend the Clio Advertising Awards ceremony, even though she pitched the original idea for the Glo Coat campaign. Fans felt Peggy's frustration at her perceived lack of recognition from Don. Further, fans pictured Peggy's feelings about the Sterling Cooper Draper Pryce (SCDP) partners inviting Joan to attend, instead of thinking to offer a ticket to Peggy. Fans struggled with emotions as if they were Peggy, as well as discussing other points of view. For example, this fan believes that Joan's being invited was more about appearance than status or merit: "Joan's presence at the Clio ceremony is a sign not of her status at SCDP but of her greater value as eye candy than Peggy, who deserved the honor more."

Fans also imagine what it must be like for Peggy, and for other women in the *Mad Men* world, as they struggle to be recognized for their own merits. Here one fan discusses the various women and the limitations for advancement:

> Don [initially] promoted Peggy to copywriter not to reward Peggy but to punish Pete. Joan was promoted to partner not because of her years of competence but because she literally whored herself out to secure an important client. Dawn is only there because the partners felt obligated to hire a black employee. Megan's promotion to copywriter, and then her first acting job, are both facilitated by her marriage to Don. Even Betty, in Season 1, is only hired as a model because the [McCann] agency . . . is trying to woo Don. The only example of a woman advancing on this show as a result of her actual work is Ted hiring Peggy at [Cutler Gleason and Chaough], and she was knocked right back down the ladder within a few episodes [due to the merger between CGC and SCDP]. Their fate is entirely subject to the whims of the men.

Viewers identified with Peggy's struggles in her romantic life as well. Our research found that fans often discussed the topic of characters choosing between career success and romantic happiness, and Peggy was a focus of these discussions. When Peggy's relationship with journalist Abe ends dramatically with her accidentally stabbing him (she thinks he is a burglar, and he takes this as a sign to break up), viewers were not upset. Instead, they hoped Peggy would develop a relationship with her colleague Stan. Unfortunately, at the end of the first half of season seven, such a relationship exists only in our minds . . . and in the fan fiction.

Instead, Peggy finds romance with her married boss, Ted Chaough. Despite the moral quandary presented by their relationship, a majority of fans were rooting for its success. Viewers felt that Ted and Peggy were a good match because they treated each other as equals and inspired each other. Yet, as with Peggy's previous married lovers — Pete and Duck — it doesn't work out with Ted. One fan imagined what Peggy goes through when Ted chooses his family, and the California office of Sterling Cooper & Partners, over the relationship he promised her:

Peggy is SO isolated — both at work and home. At the office, she has lost both of her mentors (Don and Ted) who valued her professionally and personally. Her new boss doesn't appreciate her and her coworkers laugh at her. Plus, she has no support systems either in or out of the office. She's cut her ties with her family and radical boyfriend, both of whom never respected her. No wonder she's so unhappy.

The fan consensus is that Peggy will find romantic success once she finds a partner who is her equal, regardless of whether Ted is that person.

Some viewers find that Peggy's struggle to balance work and her personal life is a realistic representation of what it's like for a woman to have a demanding career. This fan believes that Peggy's story line is believable because it is complex, sometimes dark, and feels authentic: "I think Peggy having her own personal problems in the business is one of the best things they could do. This show is no Mary Tyler Moore simple empowerment story about Peggy making it in a man's world. It's a lot of hard truth about business life and the costs it has on the people involved."

Even for fans who don't identify with Peggy, there is much concern for her character and what lies ahead for her in the final episodes. In the season seven episode "A Day's Work" it is Valentine's Day and Peggy mistakenly believes the roses on her secretary Shirley's desk are a gift for her from Ted. Due to embarrassment over her mistake, Peggy hastily demands that Shirley be reassigned.

Some fans believed that her actions in "A Day's Work" show that Peggy is becoming like Don, emulating his bad behavior and inconsiderate treatment toward subordinates. Here, a viewer talks about the implications of Peggy becoming a member of the boy's club: "I'm worried about where the show seems to be taking her. Of course there were women in that era who had success, but turned out to be drunken, bitter, heartless jerks like some of the men. . . . I just don't want Peggy to be one of them!"

The fans who theorize that Peggy's story arc will end with her becoming like Don or other male executives root their theories in historical accounts, knowing that the show's writers like to reflect history in the show. In the next excerpt a fan imagines Peggy's perspective to gain insight on her actions, preferring to see them as a misstep, rather than Peggy turning into a bully:

> Peggy is much like Don—remember he's the man who is a blank slate. Peggy, in her way, is a blank slate, too. Not as much of course. But she has to trailblaze her role and her life. In everything she has to figure out a way to do it and you can see her careening this way and that. I think she's going to figure out that playing mini-me to Don Draper isn't going to work—didn't work—and I hope there's some redemption there.

This fan addresses her hopes for Peggy in the final episodes: "I want Peggy to succeed and get over herself, but is being the future, female version of Don really the most triumphant path one can take on this show? I want to see liberation for all of the female characters (especially Joan and Sally), not just Peggy."

Fans' strong identification with Peggy and their desire for her to succeed without sacrificing herself stem from the fact that they want the same thing for themselves. An ending where Peggy becomes like Don or some of the other men on the show could be ultimately unsatisfying. Instead, an ending in which Peggy manages to retain her identity and achieve success would be a validation of the time that fans invested in rooting for her, and could in turn boost their own capacity for such success.

Betty Hofstadt Draper Francis

Fans do not fully identify with Betty like they do with Peggy. Instead, Betty serves other functions. Some are reassured that, regardless of the mistakes they made with their children, Betty has done worse. Viewers also derive pleasure from watching Betty act out. In addition to motherhood and her "bad" behavior, fans like to talk about her side of the relationship with Don.

Pop culture sites including *Vulture*, the *Daily Beast*, and the *Huffington Post* consistently named Betty Draper as one of the "Worst TV Moms." Entire articles are dedicated to Betty's worst moments as a parent, including locking Sally in a closet and telling her to go bang her head against a wall. Fans too are critical of Betty's mothering skills, finding her overly harsh in her punishments or emotionally cold and distant. Many believe Betty is a self-absorbed narcissist who only pays attention to her children when punishing them. One fan was so upset by Betty's parenting that he had to stop watching *Mad Men* entirely: "Betty Draper is a raging narcissist and the reason I had to stop watching the show a couple seasons ago. I've known mothers like her and they are hell on their kids. I either had to stop watching or risk throwing something at my TV. She's stuck as a child and can't stand anyone else getting attention."

Other fans are quick to defend Betty. Here one fan points out that today's parenting is much different from that in the *Mad Men* era: "Betty is a bit cool and aloof toward her children, but I'd say she passes the 'good enough' test for her day. All her harshness, her emotional neglect, and severe temper are no worse than the over reaction of today's stereotypical parent who is slavishly devoted to their children's every waking second."

One of the most interesting findings in our research is that fans simultaneously label Betty as "bad" while also defending her. Many fans who did not like Betty or considered her a bad mother attributed her flaws to the gender roles of the 1960s, her personality traits, and her issues with Don. For example, while fans agree that Betty was a poor example of a mother, they were quick to point out that Don was not a good father either. Here, one fan describes the complex issues that contribute to Betty's parenting approach:

> I know that she's not the best parent, but I think everyone is hard on Betty. One example of her bad parenting was locking Sally in the closet when she caught her smoking. Please . . . it was for 10 seconds, and she was trying to make an impression on the girl. I bet she did! The Betty character is a housewife who is singlehandedly raising her kids with very little input from her husband and the kids' father. There are so many other things on that show that make me laugh out loud at the absurdity of them but her parenting skills are not one of them. Sure, Don is a hottie, but would you want to be married to him? He sleeps with his daughter's teacher for crying out loud!

In contrast to the heavy media criticism of Betty, many fans point out that Don's flaws as a parent are often overlooked. In response to an article that named Betty the "Worst TV Mom," this fan pointed out the unfairness of targeting Betty while ignoring Don's parenting: "I think this article should be about Don and why he is the worst TV dad ever. There were multiple times when he wanted to ditch the family and run away. He rarely comes home and does little when it comes to parenting. I wonder why there is so much criticism of Betty when most of her problems are caused by Don."

Many fan discussions about Betty led to personal reflections and social analysis about the larger concepts of motherhood and gender roles. Fans engaging in these conversations found that Betty provided them the opportunity to think about the past and to imagine what things would have been like for young women and new mothers in the early 1960s, especially their own mothers. This fan in particular uses a scene enacted by Betty to imagine how her own mother may have reacted similarly: "I was the oldest of 7 children, a teenager in the 60s whose mom had her last child when I was 16 in 1965. After Betty Draper is home from hospital with the last baby and she wakes up to its crying and stands there. Just stands there. No matter how great a mom I had—I wondered when I saw this scene if my mom ever just stood there too."

Another fan uses her interpretation of Betty's housewife role to construct an understanding of her own mother's attitudes and behaviors:

Women during the 1960's were unfulfilled. With all due respect to my mom (I love her to bits), she like Betty Draper was a product of their generation. Women are not expected to have a life outside of the home. My mom who is now in her late seventies, to this very day tells me that she resented her mum, dad and my father. When I was growing up she was resentful that I worked and got a college education. My parents have never been the touchy-feely type of parents. They were verbally abusive . . . and that is how they were brought up. They were World War II, depression era children. *Mad Men* really helped me understand how my parent's generation really view the world.

As we know, viewers identify with fictional characters they see as heroes or as similar to themselves. Inversely, fictional characters that are seen as ethically questionable or representative of qualities that viewers do not want to associate themselves with are psychologically held at a distance. Media psychologists Elly Konijn and Johan Hoorn found that viewers who hold a certain character in low regard can remain highly involved in the character's story, even without the strong ties of identification. This may explain why so many fans are invested in Betty even though they don't identify with her. In fact, Betty's portrayal of motherhood boosted many viewers' self-esteem by offering a comparative model of parenting.

Depictions of Betty's parenting provide suspense and drama while also assuring fans that their parenting is superior. For this fan, Betty's behavior ties with only one other great viewing pleasure: "Gotta say that part of the pleasure out of watching *Mad Men* (aside from ogling Jon Hamm) is Betty's bad parenting — in comparison to Betty, I'm a really good parent."

Commenting on the "TV's Best and Worst Moms" blog (2014) this fan wrote, "Betty . . . [is] sure to assuage our guilt." As one blogger said, "Betty Draper lives so we can feel good about our parenting." In the next excerpt, a viewer (identifying herself as a stay-at-home parent) wrote about the harsh truths of motherhood and how the portrayal of Betty reflects aspects of her real life: "What I love about *Mad Men* is that it's so honest that it hurts. Watching Betty did make me cringe and think and take a hard look at myself. I think for the most part I put my daughter first, but then there are times I really want her to just nap for another 30 mins so I can get this done already!"

Other fans love Betty because they find her rash behavior — such as shooting pigeons or slapping Helen Bishop — incredibly entertaining. For these fans Betty offers a form of wish fulfillment because through her outrageous actions they vicariously experience things they could only dream of. Regardless of the time period, slapping your uppity neighbor at the grocery store, shooting your neighbor's obnoxious pets, or having post–weight loss celebratory sex with your (now remarried to a younger woman) ex-husband are all behaviors that would be considered immoral, if not illegal. But when we watch Betty do these things, it feels gratifying.

Here fans describe how the mere appearance of Betty doing outrageous things — while looking like a Barbie doll — aids in the experience of our shock: "Why not have the devil in a blonde bob? . . . Isn't Betty what great television is all about?" and "I can never look at Betty without thinking of her with a cigarette in her mouth, taking potshots at the neighbor's pigeons." Another fan describes one of their favorite scenes of Betty being bad: "The Betty— that sleeps with Don and has breakfast with Henry the next morning and is singing camp songs with [her and Don's son] Bobby—is fucking awesome."

As much as fans like to watch Betty being terrible, when it comes to her relationship with Don, many fans are quick to come to her defense. These fans generally exhibit a great deal of sympathy for her and blame Don for the state of their marriage. One fan considers Betty's perspective in addressing other fan criticisms of her quick remarriage to Henry:

> She [Betty] finds out that her husband is having an affair, she's naturally pissed and is more than ready to leave him but can't because she's pregnant and her doctor won't let her have an abortion. Do you remember how sad she was? She was angry about being cheated on, sad that she had to stay with him. . . . She got so much crap for being miserable all the time [from other fans] yet no one took a second to realize why. Or why she would fall in love with Henry so fast. . . . People thought she was so stupid for leaving Don for him but can you really blame her? . . . I don't see how she contributed to how screwed up that marriage was at all. I think she was just being a flawed human like everyone else on the show.

While fans don't necessarily find Betty very likeable, they evaluate Don's treatment of her as being much worse. Fans were especially shocked when in the second episode of the series Don called Betty's psychiatrist to get a full report on Betty's session. Fans were dismayed that the psychiatrist was willing to reveal to Don what Betty had shared, but they were more disgusted that Don would invade Betty's private confidences. Based upon Don's treatment of her, many fans began to wish that Betty would have an affair. These fans watched with hopeful anticipation when Betty flirted with the air-conditioning salesman in the season one episode "Indian Summer." Instead of having an affair, Betty utilized the washing machine for some good ~~clean~~ dirty fun.

Later on, when Betty finally had a one-night stand after learning about Don's infidelity, fans felt that Betty deserved such an experience and were happy for her:

I just hated how Don would sleep around with all these women, but would not have sex with Betty. One time he said: "Not now; it's too hot." Also, when they were going to have dinner with the comedian . . . he told her to be charming. She asked something like "Is this where I talk or stay quiet?" I really felt bad for her. She obviously was not being sexually satisfied by Don when she was mounting on top of the washer fantasizing of having sex with the salesman. . . . When the man that wasn't good at horseback riding made a move on her I kinda wanted her to go with it and have an affair with him.

In instances like this, when viewers endorse an act by a character that would typically be considered immoral, such as an extramarital affair, they engage in "moral disengagement." Fans are likely to be morally disengaged when a character is well-liked or considered to be mostly good and upstanding. In these cases the good character may have to do something bad because they have no choice or because it will result in a positive outcome. In Betty's case, though, it appears that even though fans don't necessarily see her as good or even generally likeable, they see Don's treatment of her and his behavior in their marriage as overwhelmingly poor. Thus, for fans Betty's temptation to cheat, or the actual act of cheating, is justified and even warranted.

While fans lay the blame on Don for their failed marriage, and as flawed as the characters are, a few imagine a happy ending where Betty and Don get back together. This fan believes that despite their divorce Betty and Don will always have a connection: "What a piece of work Betty is. Did you catch that child-like pout she gave when Henry was scolding her in the car for her behavior at the restaurant? She is so immature and I think Henry is good for her, but there is still a tie to Don that she can't deny. . . . It might be far fetched, but is it possible her and Don will reunite some day?" Another fan describes her own fantasy ending as being childish but happy:

But like [a] child, I hope for a Don and Betty reconciliation. In my fantasy series final season, Megan leaves Don for Hollywood. Betty takes an honest look at her marriage to Henry and decides to cut her losses. Then Don and Betty find each other again. Both of them grown enough to respect and love each other again. Yea, it's a pretty farfetched fantasy, but I still hope for the family reconciliation. If only for poor Gene [Betty and Don's youngest child], who has no memories of Mom & Dad together.

The desire fans have for fictional characters to reach positive conclusions and for their stories to have satisfactory and definitive endings is what cultural scholar Raymond Williams calls "flow." Television history has provided us with numerous examples of series endings that answer all our questions and leave us with a satisfied feeling, such as *The Wonder Years*, *Roseanne*, and *MASH*. As many *Mad Men* fans indicate, however, expecting such an ending would be "far-fetched" for *Mad Men*. Series creator Matthew Weiner has never provided either grand conclusions or even cliffhangers to *Mad Men*'s seasonal story lines.

Additionally, many fans know Weiner from his prior work on *The Sopranos*, which included a series finale characterized by media scholars as a prime example of "flow disruption." Flow disruption is when a series leaves viewers with a cliffhanger or with unresolved issues that are meant to provoke deeper-level critical thinking about a larger issue. Such endings disrupt viewer complacency. *The Sopranos* left many viewers with more questions than answers and as a result unhappy. It is in this vein that fans try to manage expectations for the final outcomes of *Mad Men*.

Megan Calvet Draper

Some fans became irritated with the amount of screen time the character of Megan was getting in seasons five and six (which included the infamous "Zou Bisou Bisou" party and Megan's return to her acting career). They felt this attention to Megan was unnecessary and detracted from other characters, such as Betty and Sally, whom they were eager to learn more about.

At the time of this fan dissent, *Vulture* magazine asked show creator Matthew Weiner why we were seeing so much of Megan. Weiner responded that every scene with Megan, regardless of whether Don is present, is about how Don will be impacted: "Megan versus work, Megan at work, and what it means to have a second wife — which he is taking very seriously as his last wife." He said that Megan serves a purpose as Don's partner and is meant to answer the important question of whether Don learned any lessons from his first marriage: "How is Don dealing with this younger, enthusiastic, hopeful, and very honest person who is accepting of the kind of person that he is but slowly expressing her independence? I found it to be a fascinating thing to say, 'How does Don deal with this successful relationship, and how much change [of Megan, and perhaps other things] can he tolerate?'"

Weiner alluded to the answer to this question in the same article, pointing out that by season five, episode ten, "Christmas Waltz," Don and Megan have had a serious argument over conflicting ideologies regarding the advertising industry, after which Don spends the afternoon literally playing at marriage with Joan as the two test drive a Jaguar and go for drinks.

As with all artistic creations, the creator's intentions aren't always reflected in viewer interpretations. An audience is a diverse body, each individual with her own life experiences that she applies as she processes the on-screen situations. This can result in a wide variety of perspectives across any fandom. However, Weiner's explanation for the heavy focus on Megan is very much in line with fan discussions—regardless of whether fans involved in these discussions are self-proclaimed as for, against, or ambivalent about Megan.

Compared to other main characters, our research revealed that there is generally less discussion dedicated solely to Megan, and much of this discussion is simply about whether or not one likes her character. When in-depth conversations about Megan happen, the focus is usually on her compatibility with Don, comparisons to Betty, and how her career goals impact her husband. As one fan wrote, "I really like Megan and don't mind all of the screen time she's getting. She is so much better of a match with Don. I don't miss bitchy, whiney, childlike Betty." Another agreed: "I'm pro Megan but . . . I hope season 5 doesn't end up feeling like 'The Megan Show.' It is interesting and a little grating how good she appears to be at everything, yet has seemed to achieve her success [and] status in life . . . marrying the rich boss. But I think that's true to life: people are handed advantages which may seem unfair, but that doesn't automatically make them unqualified, always."

Still, this conversation raises the issue again of "whose story is it anyway?" If Geppetto creates Pinocchio to be a puppet, can anyone else turn him into a real boy? In the case of *Mad Men*, can the fans do that? This is the land of story, and there's no absolute reality here. There are sets of interpretations that can be argued. Our interpretation is that whether or not Weiner intended Megan to be a vehicle for Don, fans, critics, even actress Jessica Paré who plays Megan can experience her differently. AMC certainly holds the copyright to all characters associated with *Mad Man* and can control how characters are represented in public spaces. But within the realm of our minds as viewers, no one can control the meanings that we each derive from a character and her stories.

Fans like to discuss why Don chose Megan. There is a consensus that Megan's path to Don's heart was through his children. Already his secretary, Megan is also hired to be his children's babysitter for their vacation to Disneyland at the last minute. Fans speculate that, in the beginning of their relationship, much of Don's desire for Megan stemmed from how different she was from Betty. They believe he ignored many of Megan's other characteristics in favor of the more appealing ones. Don's relationship tendencies are even called out within the show by his girlfriend Dr. Faye (a psychologist). When Dr. Faye learns from Don—via a phone call—that she is being dumped for his secretary Megan, she says that Don "only likes the beginning of things."

At least one fan endorses Dr. Faye's perspective, writing, "When he married Megan, for many viewers, her warmth and ability to get along with his kids seemed like part of her appeal. That remains true. But given the first few episodes [of season five], we see the difference in perspective between a gorgeous, gregarious and open 26-year-old (Megan) and an increasingly conservative 40-year-old (Don)." But this conflict doesn't dismay her: "But then, their relationship plays out in fascinating ways; I think (and hope) they remain together at least for a while. But 40, in 1966, was definitely 'The Establishment.' Don looks it, dresses it, acts it."

The majority of fans, even those who were displeased with Megan's screen time, were hopeful that Megan and Don's marriage would work out. "I do not understand all the Megan haters. I like her. She seems positive and alive. I think she is good for Don," one said. Yet, as Megan matured and worked toward her dreams, fans saw Don being left behind: "He loved the idea of

Megan. When he saw her care for Sally, he fell in love with the nurturing mother Megan. When she wanted her own career outside of his world, the mirage vanished."

Further, many fans drew connections between the ascent of Megan's acting career and Don's return to his old habits. "I did hate Draper at first," wrote one fan. "The way he treated Betty. . . . But . . . him being alone, trying to sober up, and then all of last season being a decent and honest man to Megan made you believe, alright, maybe he is growing and evolving." But she ended up disappointed: "Then with that one turn of the door to see his mistress at the opening of the season put it all in the trash. He's never changed. He never will. He is simply a horrible person, and what he's doing to Megan is exactly what he did to Betty. I'm so ready for Don Draper to crash."

Another fan underscored that Megan and Don's relationship had gotten off to a much better start than his marriage to Betty. "Then you've got Megan. This time, Don was upfront with her about his secret identity. But what about his real personality—the real Don underneath his persona? He never really gave that a shot and instead decided that Megan just wanted him for the money and connections he brought to the table. And, when Megan left advertising for acting, Don took it personally."

Fans are keenly aware of the fact that Megan's success means changes for Don. It is in this way that Matthew Weiner's statements about the purpose of Megan's story line are reflected in fan discussions. The juxtaposition of Megan's creative passion and Don's creative burnout also led fans to hypothesize that the seeming end of their marriage in the first half of season seven would result in Don clearing his head and "getting back to work" in the second half of the season.

Joan Holloway Harris

Fans love *Mad Men*'s office manager, and later partner, bombshell Joan. A video short, "Modern Office," created by the web site Funny or Die that features Christina Hendricks, the actress who plays Joan, attempting to complete 1960s work with 2014 technology has over 1.3 million views. Besides the humor of Joan not recognizing a modern telephone and commiserating with millennial office workers about not knowing how to fax, fans delighted in Joan for various other reasons, like . . . her . . . aesthetics.

A poll of *Esquire* magazine readers voted Christina Hendricks as the "sexiest woman in the world" in 2010. Male and female fans alike enjoy the appearance of the curvaceous actress in the role of Joan. Interestingly, that sex appeal and charisma are the reasons why Christina Hendricks got the part. She had originally received a preview script for Peggy but ended up auditioning for Midge Daniels, Don's mistress, and then for Joan.

In fact, Hendricks first thought the script for Joan sounded "bitchy." In a 2012 interview with the *Hollywood Reporter*, she said that when she auditioned for Joan she had to work at making the character real and relatable because some of the things she said were pretty harsh — such as telling Peggy to put a bag over her head and look in the mirror. In the same interview, creator Matthew Weiner said that initially Joan was only a small part, meant for infrequent appearances. But after Hendricks brought a cerebral and physical chemistry to the scenes with other characters, the role expanded into that of a main character.

And thank goodness! Without Joan fans could not discuss all of the important aspects of her story line — her love life, her career trajectory, and most importantly, the scandalous move that made her partner.

According to our research conversations about Joan frequently focus on her relationship with Roger, both in the beginning of the series and later, when their son Kevin is born. One fan compares Joan and Roger's relationship to real-life office affairs of the bygone era: "Not that you'd ever see that in a personnel manual, but it wasn't unusual for a secretary to 'take care of' her boss in many ways. Look at Joan and Roger. That relationship changes over time, and Joan comes out triumphant (last night was particularly sweet [with her promotion to the upstairs office]!) and Roger is just . . . sad in his over-occupied bed."

Joan and Roger's affection for each other throughout the series — even when not together romantically — had many fans theorizing that perhaps in the end Joan and Roger would end up together. Of course, this is a nice thought given that they have a secret child together. Much like the desire that fans have for a Betty/Don reconciliation, a happy ending for Joan and Roger would satisfy our desire for the flow of happy closure. Though much like the Peggy/Ted romance, fans acknowledged the moral issues of Joan and Roger's office-based romance: both are married to other people.

Fans experienced moral disengagement about Joan and Roger's affair, feeling that love was more important than their unhappy marriages. Viewers often see the flaws of the characters and their unique situations as creating gray areas between right and wrong. Instead of being morally good, we would rather see these characters as happy and fulfilled. For example, one fan says that she felt good that Roger had fathered Joan's son: "I don't think Joan and Roger are very sad—I don't know why, I probably should! They have a strange connection that underlies all their interactions, and I think they genuinely will always care for each other. And is it weird I'm glad Joan had his baby?" Another viewer finds a Joan and Roger relationship more satisfying given the quality of their other romantic partners: "Actually, I miss Joan and Roger together. How many more idiots will they both have to sleep with until they finally end up together?"

It's not hard to understand why viewers prefer a Joan/Roger pairing. The only other long-term relationship we've seen her in is with her husband, Greg Harris. In season two, after a visit to the office where Joan introduces then-fiancé Greg to Roger and others, Greg rapes her on the floor of Don's office. Following this event, fans were solidified in their disgust for Greg and their sympathy for Joan. Many referred to Greg Harris as "Dr. Rapist" or as "Joan's Rapist Husband." This viewer perceives Joan's choice to marry Greg anyway as going along with social expectations and the desire to attain the status of being a doctor's wife, rather than create a scandal by breaking off their engagement: "Joan . . . gave in and got married to [the] 'good catch' doctor who date-raped her!"

Much like Betty and Don's superficial marriage, Joan's is not a happy one. In the season three episode "The Gypsy and the Hobo," fans immensely enjoyed a scene where an irate Joan smashed a lamp on her husband's head after he asked her if she understood what it was like to want something she couldn't have. Here one fan describes her response while watching this scene: "I loved what Joan did. I'd love to smash a vase over a rapist's head. . . . I don't

Figure 14. Greg Harris, fiancé of Joan Holloway, rapes her on
the floor of Don Draper's office after she shows him around
the building (screen capture from season two, episode 12,
"The Mountain King").

care if it's in self-defense, three weeks later, or in several decades. Smash away,
Joan."

Another fan was so gratified by this scene that she experienced both emotional and physical responses: "That was just so cathartic to see. When it first
happened I actually said, 'Holy shit!' out loud, absolutely stunned . . . then
I was overjoyed. I think it's because, in their scenes together, there always
seems to be this tension, this underlying threat of danger from Greg. . . . I'm
always kind of on the edge of my seat with them." Fans were pleased when
Greg was quickly dispatched to war and out of the story line, letting Joan's
story of independence come into the spotlight.

Fans find Joan smart and capable, characterizing her as an unintentional
career woman. Instead of identifying with her, as they do with Peggy, fans
see Joan as a representation of what it would have been like for a woman
to make partner when women were still largely limited to pink-collar jobs.
Peggy's career trajectory represents the exception, while Joan's represents the
historical ways that a woman had to get ahead. Viewers are especially concerned with her evolution across the series. Fans believe that her transformation from seeking to land a good husband to negotiating a partnership
evolved out of opportunity and necessity.

In the season five episode "The Other Woman," Joan, now a single mother, gets a unique opportunity to solidify her place in the company when the head of Jaguar indicates that he will give the firm his business if she will agree to spend the night with him. All of the partners approach Joan about this, offering her a bonus, with the exception of Don, who finds the entire suggestion distasteful. Partner Lane Pryce, who has a close working relationship with Joan, privately encourages her to seek a partnership share in the agency instead, indicating that it will result in greater financial stability.

Fans passionately debated Joan's choice to exchange sex for a partnership. Some believe, given the options in society for a woman in the 1960s, it was a small sacrifice to make for a long-term gain in security for herself and her son: "I thought of Joan as doing this . . . for her job but she also could have been thinking about the welfare of her and her baby's future."

A few viewers found the story line sensational and unrealistic, while others had similar stories to share about real-life sexual propositions and exploitation they experienced. Interestingly, Matthew Weiner has said that Joan's story line was rooted in stories he heard from people who had worked on Madison Avenue in the 1960s.

Lynn Spigel's research has shown that fans can still use fictional events to make sense of claims about progress and modernity even if they don't find them entirely believable. For fans, Joan's sex-based transaction served as a comparative index for measuring social progress, including the liberation of women, and especially the ascension of women to the highest positions within companies. For example, fans believed that Joan's work on its own deserved a promotion, but that during the *Mad Men* era merit would not have been enough to earn a partnership for a woman.

Fans acknowledge that, in comparison to today's procedures for advancement, Joan's breaking of the glass ceiling would have been very rare:

Joan was made a partner because she compromised herself for the "company good" and the other partners all knew it. They didn't feel that she was their equal in spite of her new title. She wasn't even on the partner's floor. Knowing all she knows, and with her quick mind, she's probably the smartest of the bunch. Let's hope she now gets the respect she deserves.

Following this episode, fans compared the work-related advantages of Peggy's and Joan's sexual relationships. Some fans argued that, while Peggy is no stranger to sleeping with men in her office or the industry (Pete, Duck, Ted), such relationships have been just that—actual relationships, rather than sexual transactions. Joan and Peggy both work hard in their positions, but Joan's ascension is a move that many viewers feel would have been impossible without sex. Some fans worry that this transaction diminishes the value of Joan's position and that it will undermine her reputation and power. But Joan makes the most of what she's gained.

Once she is a partner, Joan takes matters into her own hands to land the Avon account and become an account manager. Here a fan compares Joan's attitudes and aspirations from season one to her keeping the Avon account for herself (and from an irritated Pete) in season six: "Keep in mind that in Season 1 Joan . . . believed she had achieved as much as she could and no woman there [at the firm] could achieve more. She constantly reminded Peggy of her place [as a secretary]. Only recently had she realized she could do more because Peggy proved it."

In the season seven episode "A Day's Work," Joan moves to an upstairs office, the floor where all the other partners are located, and passes her duties as head of personnel to Dawn, one of the two black secretaries at the agency. Fans were pleasantly surprised by this event and also considered it a bold move, given the lingering racism in the office. Here a fan expresses her excitement at Joan's promotion: "I must say that she will be fabulous in her new position, however, once and *if* she's able to get past others' perceptions of her. She's one very smart cookie."

(Anyone else think Joan would love to give ditzy Meredith the boot ASAP? Crude cartoonist Joey and former flame Paul Kinsey should probably thank their lucky stars they are no longer office fixtures.)

Sally Beth Draper

Fans love to talk about Sally. While the show is populated by many grown-ups, Sally is the character we've watched grow from a five-year-old girl to a teenager on the cusp of adulthood. Fans enjoy discussing Sally as a product of her parents, how the character serves to expose the hypocrisy of adults around her, and imagining her life as an adult.

Beginning in the early seasons, Sally is a source of great concern for fans. Much of that concern is rooted in how her parents' actions affect her and how they may shape who she becomes. Fans draw connections between Sally's attitudes and beliefs and how these things are derived either from Don or Betty. Or sometimes viewers see Sally's behavior as something she has actively selected to distinguish herself from her parents.

Fans see Sally's personality traits and actions as a blend of her parents, rather than representative of just one of them. Interestingly, no one attributes these things as belonging to her solely or to another influential adult figure such as Henry, Megan, or a teacher. Typically, when we see her parents reflected in Sally, the traits are negative.

"Sally is an interesting mix of both parents," wrote one fan. "She has her mother's ability to manipulate people. Some of the mannerisms and expressions portrayed by her are pure Betty. Some of her actions are more like Don; they both invented fake names—Don to leave his old life behind, Sally to buy beer. They both tried to run away—Don joined the army, and Sally tried to take the train without paying."

Another viewer agrees, saying he finds Sally's blend of characteristics horrifyingly entertaining: "When Sally was in the boarding school and Glen [her friend] started hilariously beating up his friend, Sally has this little smirk on her face. That reminded me of the smirk Don gave when Roger blew chunks in the lobby in season one. The smirk was Don, the manipulation of Glen was Betty. She truly is Frankenstein's Monster."

When Sally lies about tripping her stepgrandmother with a telephone cord Sally had stretched across the room—the girl claimed the culprit was a toy, one fan blamed Don's approach to truth telling: "Sally's a pathological liar just like daddy. How sweet." Another viewer took into consideration Sally's motivation to lie: "With a mother like Betty, any kid would learn to lie as a survival technique." He makes a good point, after all, since we know that Betty's past punishments include getting locked in a closet or slapped.

In addition to seeing the way that children reflect their parents, viewers find that Sally serves to expose the hypocrisy of the world and, more spe-

Figure 15. Sally Draper attends a fancy American Cancer Society
event with Don, Megan, Roger Sterling, and Megan's parents,
Emile and Marie Calvet, but only after her father requests she
change out of her go-go boots and remove her makeup. Later Sally
witnesses Roger and Marie engaged in "dirty" acts (screen capture
from season five, episode seven, "At the Codfish Ball").

cifically, the adults around her. In season five, episode seven, "At the Codfish Ball," she attends an event thrown by the American Cancer Society
with Don, Megan, Megan's parents Marie and Emile, and Roger Sterling.
In comparison to other episodes that offer only small scenes with Sally, she
is a major focus of this one. This episode was an emotional roller coaster for
viewers, who were excited for Sally's night out and later distressed by the
night's events.

Fans compared her appearance early in the episode to Betty and noted
Don's poignant response to her as she modeled her outfit for him. Don's request that Sally remove the adult makeup and go-go boots she first wore was
a significant scene for one fan, causing her to see Sally as Don does, and to
see Don genuinely impacted: "Above all else, don't forget to say things like
this to your sweet baby girl before she grows up and becomes an adult: 'You
know what makes me happy? A beautiful young lady who will someday be
wearing makeup. But not tonight.' Once in a very great while, Don Draper
really is a good dad."

Another viewer considered what Don may have felt when he saw Sally,
describing the similarity between Sally and Betty, but focusing this time on

appearance rather than character traits: "When I saw her appear in her top knot, it reminded me of the updo Bets wore when she and Don were in Italy. I thought that is what Don may have been reacting to — Sally looking too much like Bets."

Fan conversations about this portion of the episode focused closely on the perceptions of parent-child relationships and the important things parents can do or say that have a lingering impact on their children. Further, viewers were genuinely touched by twelve-year-old Sally's excitement at being included in the grown-ups' fun, which made what happened later in the episode especially deflating. Viewers were shocked at the tween's glimpse of Marie and Roger in mid-fellatio. Fans felt crushed for Sally — who went in a single day from dreaming of fairytale ballrooms to witnessing extramarital sex acts.

One viewer points out the juxtaposition of Sally's excitement and desire to be included in the adult world with the shocking reality of seeing adults in action: "The entire evening was holding so much promise: . . . Sally in her new mod outfit getting a chance to be grown-up at a big deal for her Dad, and then gets a shocking grown-up eyeful with 'date' Roger and her step-grandmother, no less."

Another perceives Sally's letdown as a reflection of the various adults' experiences that night — that if Sally hadn't seen Roger and Marie, her experience would have retained that exciting childlike wonder of the adult world. Instead, she sees that being a grown-up is nothing like she imagined, and in fact, may not be something she is ready for:

Mad Men uses a smartly constructed cross-generational arc to demonstrate the adage "be careful what you wish for." It was demonstrated skillfully with Sally, who is buoyed by Roger's non-condescending charm and allowed to feel "adult" despite her father's demand that she take off her makeup and switch out of her go-go boots. And then she's faced with the same buzz-kill as all the adult characters [from other circumstances that night] upon seeing Roger . . . in an "adult" circumstance that compromises her evening out as an adult "equal."

Another fan echoes this sentiment about Sally's education in adult activities: "Do you remember when, after she caught Roger with Megan's mom Marie, she spoke with Glen who was away at prep school? Glen asked Sally 'How was New York?' and Sally answered, 'Dirty.' It was the last line of the episode and it was a 'Bam!' moment."

Our concern for Sally peaks again following the season six episode "Favors," when the girl catches her father having sex with Sylvia Rosen. Fans are quick to sympathize with Sally's outraged response. Again, Sally enables us to see the difference between what children are told is right and the hypocritical behavior that adults engage in. "The scene where Don is caught by Sally was huge, even if it was unsubtle in its set up," one fan argued. "I think it's the tip over point for Don. . . . Your kids realizing you're a human being is one thing, but them thinking you're a bad human being is another." Another sympathizes with the teenager: "As for Sally . . . man, it's rough. Ice Queen Betty or Don Dick Cheating I-Have-No-People Whitman Draper Lying Liarface? It's a wonder she even seems as well adjusted as she does. God, she was so broken at the dinner table [after seeing Don and Sylvia], and I realized then that she's not grown up, that we've watched Sally grow up literally in front of our eyes, but she's also . . . still a little girl."

Fans recognize that traumatic events can shape our lives and serve as pivotal points that change everything that happens afterward. For this fan, Sally walking in on Don cheating is one of those events: "In our lives most of us have 3 or 4 traumatic 'before and after' moments. As Sally gets older, she will quantify things that happen in her life as before I saw my father having sex with the neighbor and after I saw my father having sex with the neighbor."

As these quotations reveal, viewers are incredibly invested in Sally and strongly desire to understand how Sally's childhood will impact her adult life, especially whether she will be strong enough to withstand her parents' often poor role modeling. "With Don's treatment of women it will be interesting to see where it takes him and Sally," said one. Some fans fear that as the product of an appearance-obsessed mother and an identity-conflicted father, Sally will become a tragedy as an adult. "Sally is likely going to become promiscuous" was the opinion of another fan. "Her dad showers more attention on 'looser' women than on . . . 'virtuous' ones. She might end up pregnant as well, which will send Betty to the bat farm." And there are worse options: "Or perhaps she becomes a hooker, like Don's mother and stepmother, completing the vicious cycle of the women in Don's life. This could contrast well with the advances the other women are making in the workplace. The '70s are coming right up for Sally, and her rebellion is just starting to take hold."

In fact, fans are so interested in what will happen to Sally as an adult that they (jokingly) propose a spinoff with an elderly Sally having flashbacks to her teen and young adult years. "Maybe they could do a spin-off set in the present day with 58-year-old Sally as the matriarch of her own brood—and fill in the gaps from her formative and young adult years?" Responded a commenter, "That would be perfect. Sally goes to California to be a hippy." But the current story line leaves another fan to lament that she won't be able to see Sally in such a setting: "I'm most sad that we won't follow Sally into young adulthood."

Perhaps these fans are on to something: a spinoff in which Sally is the creative director of an all-female design firm in the eighties, called *Designing Women*. Wait, that show was already done in the eighties! (If you are unfamiliar with it—we highly recommend you check this show out, for the sake of posterity of all things eighties.)

The desire to know what lies ahead for Sally and for all the show's characters is a testament to our transportation into the world of *Mad Men*. We are emotionally invested in these characters and what becomes of them. We want closure for the characters. We want to see what life is like for Sally as a grown-up. Will she escape the demons of her parents? And will she bypass the limitations of the women who surround her as she enters adulthood in a new era?

CHAPTER SIX

The Measure of a Mad Man

If you're old enough to remember the classic TV show *All in the Family*, or to have watched the reruns, you'll recall the famous intro scene where beloved characters Archie and Edith Bunker sit at the piano singing "Those Were the Days." Archie and Edith reminded us that "you knew who you were then: girls were girls and men were men" back in the good old days. Echoing this sentiment, a fan comments on the YouTube video of Megan Draper singing "Zou Bisou Bisou" at Don's birthday party, indicating that Megan's sexually charged performance reminds them of "a time when women were women and men were men."

But what does it mean to be a man? For creator Matthew Weiner, from the very start Don Draper was crafted as the embodiment of conflicting American ideals about manhood. Weiner joked with Stephen Colbert that "Don smoked, banged everything on the Eastern Seaboard . . . and California, sold some soap . . . was grim about it, and smoked some more." When Colbert asked Weiner if Don was designed as " a criticism of the American male," Weiner replied:

> I always sort of saw it that he was about the sort of split message that the American male gets. That you are told that you, to be attractive, on the one hand you have to be, like, you know, Little League coach, and PTA guy, great husband, great dad; on the other hand, you are supposed to smoke as much, drink as much and get laid as much as possible. Those two messages are being sent at the same time. . . . And also be winning at work.

From these comments it seems that Weiner cast Don Draper as a man in a no-win situation, his metaphorical tattoo reading "born to be torn." Should Don be a swell guy, a great dad, and a loving husband? Or should he be Dapper Dan, cigarette and scotch in one hand and a blonde in the other? Clearly, in the beginning Don fully committed to both the soft and the hard image of a man in the 1960s. Perhaps Weiner was telling us that this was the real shaft that men of the sixties dealt with.

Of course, in Don's case we have to wonder if he ever had a chance to succeed. Yes, perhaps he struggled with the impossible social mores, like other men did. But what foundation did he have to build any functional identity on? Born Dick Whitman, his childhood circumstances were horrific in Dickensian proportions. Add to that impossible beginning the trauma and shame that came with his experiences in Korea, and fans wonder how Don can end any way but in tragic self-destruction.

We found that fans lament, almost as if in Greek chorus, the depth of Don's brokenness. Yet, we see something in Don — some spark of goodness — that keeps us ever hoping against hope that he will somehow make it right.

Fans on Don and Beliefs About Masculinity

As you know, our research draws on data from thousands of fan comments posted on social media. These posts represent a new era of social science in action because we are not dragging college sophomores into a lab and forcing answers out of them. Instead, we get the good stuff — the stuff that fans volunteered because they care and because they enjoy being in community with others who also watch and think about *Mad Men*.

So, what exactly *do* all these fans say about Don from the perspective of understanding masculinity and how to be a man? Much like Matthew Weiner's interview naming the facets of masculinity, including family, sex and sexuality, and work success, fans evaluate Don on the same characteristics. Fans love Weiner's vision of Don when he is making waves at work and producing breathtaking and clever advertising. As Don becomes darker and his struggles get the best of him, we admire him less and cringe at his missteps. Instead, we watch to celebrate the successes of the other characters. We are ever hopeful that Don will recover but certainly do not hold our breath. While we wait to see what becomes of Don, fan discussions about him focus on his roles as a father and spouse. Fans see these areas as having the potential to save him.

As you read in the prior chapters, fans and media critics alike heavily criticized Betty as a parent. Yet, our research of online fan commentaries found

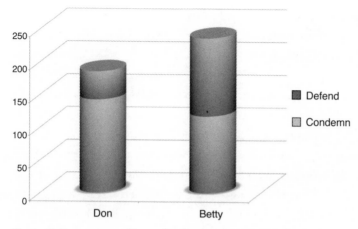

Figure 16. Comparison of how often fans condemn and defend Don
and Betty Draper in online comments. Don receives more condemning
judgments from fans than Betty, despite more negative media criticism
of Betty's character.

Don subject to far more criticism as a parent than Betty was. (And really, it's
not hard to condemn someone who failed to bring home your birthday cake
or sleeps with your teacher!) In figure 16 you can see a comparison of how
fans were evaluating Don and Betty as parents. The comments that follow in
this chapter are excerpts from those counted in the chart.

One fan says that it is easy for her to condemn Don based on his parenting. She also muses that the type of abandonment Don engages in is more
often associated with fathers, rather than mothers, in real life. In this type
of situation, much like the negative assessment of Betty by media bloggers,
social punishments for such actions differ according to the gender of the parent—letting men off the hook with a shrug while blaming women for causing
the downfall of society.

He [Don] left during his child's birthday party and didn't come back for
days. The two weeks in California where he was just gone . . . I remember
watching *Kramer vs. Kramer* with my ex-boyfriend. He was so appalled
that Meryl Streep's character just up and left her child and at how much
of a hard time Dustin Hoffman's character had adjusting to her absence.

I thought, men do this every. single. day. In fact, your dad did this to your mom. It doesn't excuse it but the level of hate toward women or mothers who misbehave is unfair.

Another fan points out the gendered discrepancies in the way that people evaluate Don and Betty's parenting. She laments that Sally favors Don and that the girl's preference translates to other fans and media critics singling out Betty for poor parenting. If you are Sally, getting a dog or Beatles tickets is exciting and can make you forget about your missing birthday cake or your parents' divorce. "What's troubling is how Don and Betty are perceived/written so differently, when it comes to parenting. They're both terrible, yet he seems to come out above the harsher criticism [from media critics]. Even allowing him to provide the gesture of Beatles tickets for Sally let him slightly off the hook."

Many fans feel that Don's role as a father is of the utmost importance and also the aspect of his life that many think can help Don sort out his other issues and gain focus. Here, the idea of conclusive flow, which we introduced in chapter 5, comes in. For Don, our flawed protagonist, fans believe there must be something that will change him, make him better, and thus allow us to feel closure. Fans suggest that one of the most compelling stories in *Mad Men* is about the journey that Don takes in becoming a good father, that it is a learning experience for his character.

"Don's children are his one shot at redemption," one fan wrote. "If it happens (which I don't think is a certainty, though I'm certainly rooting for it), it is through them that he will understand he is capable of feeling unconditional love, and being loved unconditionally in return." The importance of fatherhood was particularly clear when Don called Megan after he had given up his transfer to the California office to Ted Chaough in the season six finale "In Care Of." This phone call comes at the end of the day, when Don made inappropriate revelations during the Hershey's meeting about growing up in a whorehouse. Due to that situation, he has been drinking heavily, and now he must call Megan in California to tell her he can't move there. During the call Don cites his children as a reason for staying in New York. The same fan continued, "He is only just now beginning to realize this [how important his children are] — that is what his drunken confession to Megan was. He does love his kids but he does not know how to show or express it. In turn, he does not know how to accept it, and accepting unconditional love is a powerful and humbling thing."

Don's attitudes and behaviors when it comes to parenting draw a great deal of attention from fans. They often find him lacking in these areas, but some blame the traditions of the era or alternatively Don's personality. Fans also draw comparisons to the altered expectations of fatherhood today. For example, one fan views Don within the context of the sixties as well as having a flawed set of personal values. He explains that his view of Don is partially rooted in a real-world understanding of the time period, where, for men, providing financially was the most important responsibility of a father: "Don doesn't make his children his first priority, because as the man in the household his first priority is providing for them through work. . . . The character motivation related to the time period is fairly obvious." He also says that Don has a desire to connect emotionally with his family but that his work priorities and extramarital sexual relationships result in a cycle of emotional and physical distance from Betty and his kids: "I think that's why Don is so miserable: . . . I think whenever he neglects his family, it's him feeling guilty. Like he can't look at them knowing that he's been with other women. It's sad how it's such a vicious circle and it hurts the people he loves the most."

Another commenter compares fatherhood during the 1960s to modern parenting. She sees *Mad Men* as an accurate reflection of history — "Of course Don is an awful husband and father but men ruled in that day" — and also as a benchmark for measuring how things have changed — "They still rule but are trying to be more politically correct now. That's why I love that show because it makes us graphically look at ourselves." She believes that contemporary men still have gains to achieve in the roles of husbands and fathers: "I love taking that look back to see we've come a long way but we're not there yet." Unfortunately, she doesn't elaborate as to what those changes might be.

In figure 17 we see Don with his three children as he opens a birthday gift from them in his New York apartment. Those times when Don has special moments with his children or moments of failure result in strong emo-

Figure 17. Don receives a fortieth birthday gift from his children, Sally, Bobby, and baby Gene, during his weekend to have them. Scenes that include Don and all of his children are fairly rare across the series but high in emotional impact for fans (screen capture from season five, episode one, "A Little Kiss — Part 1").

tional experiences for fans. In these scenes fans more closely identify with the child — usually Sally — rather than Don. This fits with the findings detailed in chapter 5 where fans typically identify with other female characters (including Sally), rather than Don. In Don's interactions with his family, fans picture themselves as the child experiencing the scene, empathizing with Sally or Bobby, and ultimately they evaluate Don not just as a bad father, but also as a bad person.

The season six episode "The Flood" gave fans another opportunity to criticize Don's relationship with his children, in this case his son Bobby. In this episode Bobby tells his father that he is worried that stepfather Henry may be in danger due to the New York riots (following the assassination of Dr. Martin Luther King, Jr.). Several fans identify with Bobby and condemn Don's response as further proof of his terrible parenting and negative personality: "If Don has a compassionate and empathetic son it's because Henry is raising him for the most part," complained one. "That becomes obvious when we find out what Bobby's fear is . . . that something bad would happen to Henry. Just when Don's brain seems to be connecting to his heart, the old Whitman/Draper ego surfaces yet again, when he tells Bobby that nothing bad will happen because Henry isn't that important . . . yikes! The Draper children are doomed no matter what!"

Fans feel that Don missed opportunities to make connections with his kids due to his own shortcomings. And Bobby isn't the only Draper child who fans think is shortchanged by Don's insensitivity and inability to connect emotionally. In the season six, episode eleven "Favors," Sally walks in on her father having sex with upstairs neighbor Sylvia Rosen. It's a horrible moment for her, and fans are scathing about how Don handles it. "'I was comforting Mrs. Rosen.' Who does Don think he's talking to, a 3 year old? Sally is 14 and knows exactly what she saw. I'm afraid Don has completely ruined an already shaky relationship with his daughter now." Another fan focuses on what the moment means for Don: "The scene where Don is caught by Sally was huge, even if it was unsubtle in its set up. I think it's the tip over point for Don, and like you said, you never need to see Sylvia again after that. Your kids realizing you're a human being is one thing, but them thinking you are a bad human being is another." This fan went on, "My wife gave me a pretty intense look after that scene, and I wisely joked that I would do my best to cheat on her without the children finding out. Ah, good times sleeping on the couch."

From these comments it is clear that fans find much of Don's behavior as a parent and as a human lacking. With Betty, fans were quick to point out positive aspects to balance out her negatives. In our research, only a small handful of fans (17 of 300 comments focused on parenting) defended Don's parenting in some form. One wrote, "I always like Don's scenes with his kids. He obviously loves his kids and sometimes that is his one redeeming quality." But another countered, "He only loves his kids when they are in front of him. That doesn't mean he's a good dad."

Similar to the discussions about Betty, fans who defended Don sometimes also condemned him in the same discussion for different reasons. For example, one fan thought that overall Don was better than Betty at connecting with their children but worse in connecting with his spouse: "I think Don Draper is actually a good father. Emotionally he connects with his kids better than Betty does. He's just a lousy husband. But you know that I know a lot of guys even in this day and age who are like that: great with their kids yet can't stand their wives for whatever reason."

As these comments show, fans evaluate Don's commitment and responsibilities to his family from the perspective of being a good husband. Fans overwhelmingly blame Don for the downfall of both his marriages, and we quoted fans who defended both Betty (wife number two) and Megan (wife number three). Because, honestly, how *does* he expect to stay married when he's having extramarital sex and keeping identity secrets?

But there was that small portion of fans (about 1 percent) who found reasons to excuse or explain Don's behavior as a husband: "I think it's lame to give Betty a part in Don's infidelity. Don would cheat on any woman he ends up with. Those mommy issues are deep seeded." This fan and many others diagnose Don's troubles with emotional connections, and his addiction to sex and alcohol, as being rooted in his childhood experiences. However, most people do not take the position that this trauma excuses his behavior; rather, they feel that it simply explains it and paints him as a damaged human.

Rather than blame Don's mother, another fan charted the character's degeneration over the course of the series: "I've been re-watching Seasons 1–3 . . . and it's really striking the way the old Don was much kinder to his wife and children and how much BETTER he was at his job." In those earlier episodes, "he was troubled, but he wasn't broken. It was almost as if his bad behavior was passive, just him moving from event to person to experience in hopes something would make him feel better, and you wanted him to work through whatever it was he was going through."

This perspective is common. In early seasons fans found Don and his lifestyle glamorous, but as the series progressed and Don's life spiraled downward in many ways, fan conversations evolved. Many who coveted Don's life, including the morally questionable aspects, only did so when he was excelling in his work at the firm. As the story line advanced and Don started to fall off the wagon both professionally and literally, the admiration and aspirations to emulate him quickly diminished.

In fan conversations Don went from being labeled a "cad" whose work successes and creativity deserved admiration to being a figure to pity. Fans increasingly talked about how low he had gone, how severe his addictions had become, and whether (and how) Don might recover before the series concluded. For fans, Don's worth as a man stems mainly from his career; without that they see him as a failure as a man.

While Don has spiraled downward in the opinion of fans, another character has firmly secured a place in our hearts by exemplifying the characteristics that fans associate with popular masculinity. Which characters do fans identify as our favorite "good men"? (Hint—it's not Pete!)

Defining a "Good Man"

Fans like to invoke feminist theory when analyzing the purpose of Don's character. They believe that Don is meant to be a prefeminist embodiment of a traditional male — one who is entitled and self-absorbed, concerned only with appearances, and ultimately slow to keep up as the world around him changes. Additionally, as seasons progressed many fans were displeased with Don's actions and saw them as being at odds with what they consider to be a good man (a genuine or "real" man). We wondered what characteristics or actions fans thought were the foundational principles of being such a man. The answer appears to be a fan consensus naming the character Ken Cosgrove as the best representation of a good man on *Mad Men*.

You may recall that our first introduction to Ken — described in chapter 5 where he is sexually harassing Peggy in the elevator and planning Pete's bachelor party at the Slipper Room — is not so appealing. But he changes for the better. One fan describes the evolution of Ken's boys-club behavior in that first elevator scene in season one to season five, when Ken and Peggy successfully pitch to a client together: "I just watched the first episode from season one (trying to get my Mom to watch the show) and it was Cosgrove who was lewdly eyeing Peggy in the elevator with the verbal entendres. And now the platonic hug. You've come a long way, baby!"

Another fan reflects on that same scene. She compares Ken's positive and sincere treatment of Peggy to what the scenario would have been like if a different character — the ever-petulant Pete — were in the same situation: "I also liked the part where Peggy was out pitching for business with Ken Cosgrove,

Figure 18. Ken Cosgrove comforts long-time coworker Joan Harris after SCDP partner Lane Pryce is found dead in his office. Fans label Ken as one of the few good men on the show, citing his high regard of work relationships with Joan and Peggy — while other men are lecherous or exploitive — as being one of his best qualities (screen capture from season five, episode twelve, "Commissions and Fees").

and when they won the account, they shared a big hug — that feels contrastingly light, pleasant and uncomplicated. Cannot imagine Peggy doing the same with Pete at all, even if they did not sleep together or [Peggy] have his baby." Fans are quick to note that Ken often demonstrates compassion for his female coworkers while maintaining a professional relationship, as we see in figure 18, where he comforts a distraught Joan.

Ken, played by actor Aaron Staton, even physically embodies the boy-next-door appearance with his sandy-blond hair, easy smile, and clean-cut appearance. (In fact, Staton was tapped for the videogame L.A. Noire as the voice and physical model for the main character — a "good cop" detective.) Fans indicate that Ken's attitudes and behaviors following that initial season one debauchery — being a supportive coworker and a loving husband, desiring a work-life balance, and declining to engage with Pete's competitive challenges — paint him as a responsible, ethical, wise man.

Interestingly, *Mad Men* never offers us an explanation for Ken's transformation after his season one antics. Perhaps Matthew Weiner needed a character to provide the contrast to Don and the other misbehaving men, and Ken had been marginal enough to make such a transformation believable. (Clearly Pete was not an option!) "While Ken Cosgrove obviously isn't 'a strong counterpoint' to Don in terms of screen time or overall importance, it occurs to me that he is by far the most morally-level and well-adjusted character on *Mad Men*," one fan wrote. Or perhaps we are supposed to infer that Ken became a changed man in the space between season one and season three when his character's story line was absent. Regardless, fans immediately picked up on Ken as our ultimate golden ~~boy~~ man. This fan wrote, "We keep expecting people not to be decent. Having someone [Ken Cosgrove] being fundamentally decent is almost a fake out." The consensus among fans is that a good man is ultimately the equivalent of being a good person.

Since many fans believe that Don is a prefeminist embodiment of masculinity, it seems apt that they cast Ken as the embodiment of evolving gender roles. Specifically, fans notice and appreciate that he values the contributions of women such as Peggy in the workplace and sees his wife as more than a status symbol, housekeeper, or business connection (in contrast to how Pete uses his wife, Trudy). For fans Ken is a role model of a new type of masculinity. "I kind of like that three seasons in, Cosgrove is still just 'that really talented guy in the office,'" one fan wrote. "The only depth we get on him is that he really is as good as he seems."

In addition to admiring Ken, a few fans also named Betty's second husband, Henry Francis, as exhibiting the characteristics of a rational and supportive "good man." Indeed, Ken and Henry are among the few characters whom fans describe as true grown-ups. One contributor to a conversation about these characters said, "Agreed about Ken Cosgrove. He also seems to be happily married with a wife who both supports his interests and has her own career. Henry is also a grown-up, and I suspect Dawn [a secretary at the firm] will emerge as one, too." In contrast, this fan did not seem so sure that two major female characters would succeed in this way: "I find it interesting to watch both Joan and Peggy struggle separately with how to become executives/leaders — there are no guidebooks for them to follow."

While fans frequently compare Don to Ken, and Don to Henry, other male characters are also frequently contrasted with Ken, the ultimate example. Take Ted Chaough, best known for his one-night stand with Peggy and subsequent decision to return to his wife and stay in his marriage, rather than continue a relationship with Peggy: "Ted fancies himself a Ken Cosgrove man of integrity and morals. NOT! There's only one Ken."

Other fans argue that Ted desperately wants to be good man. Many of the conversations about Ted put his desire to be morally upstanding as being at odds with his heart. Fans believe that Ted loves Peggy and would like to leave his marriage to be with her but think his desire to be a good husband and father—and morally upstanding—prevents him from following through. In the opinion of one, "I think Ted's ego ended his relationship with Peggy. He can't stand the thought of himself as a bad guy. By dumping her, he can pretend he's on the moral high ground." Another agreed that his moral fiber just wasn't strong enough for him to buck public opinion: "He was just back to his pragmatic, semi-moral self and knew he couldn't do that to his wife. Peggy—really if she knew him should have known he would not be a man to leave his wife and kids. But they got lost in the moment and bright lipstick. That's how I took it. Peggy and the lace bra, wowza!"

This is where it gets interesting. Fans see Ted's decision to return to his family as an effort to be morally good after he has been bad by cheating with Peggy. Yet, as we've noted before, many would also like to see Ted and Peggy end up together. Fans are clear about what constitutes the morally superior choice but are also willing to root for a morally imperfect happiness over a morally ideal *un*happiness for the characters they care about.

In evaluating the struggles of a range of male characters to be good men, fans continue to use Ken as their yardstick. As one said, "There is no reward for trying to be a better person. You do it because you want to (Ken Cosgrove). Don't expect something to happen one day that completely alters your perception and habits. Change takes effort—it entails a constant, conscious struggle against your demons (Ted Chaough)." Other characters, by contrast, opt for instant gratification and fail to improve themselves, as the same writer observed: "Because after a while, as Roger discovers with LSD and Don discovers with Megan, the initial effects of event-triggered happiness wear off. What do you do then? This leads into the next point.—People don't change."

It is clear that fans have come to an overall consensus that morality is the primary characteristic that defines manhood, but they also agree that morality can be a gray area. Just as in real life, morals are negotiated in the process of living. Additionally, fans associate a lack of ego and positive treatment of women with the idea of being a good man. This is very much a post-second-wave feminist view of masculinity and, more generally, humanity.

Fans find these preferred masculine values are most embodied in the characters of Ken Cosgrove, Henry Francis, and even in some of the efforts demonstrated by Ted Chaough. Fans also concede that Don and some others are struggling to become better men. But there is one character who they agree is unable to achieve manhood, a man who is a perpetual child due to his behavior and attitudes. In the next section we talk about the characteristics of a man trapped in boyhood.

The Man-Child

In the premiere episode, "Smoke Gets in Your Eyes," Don Draper tells his mistress Midge about the kid who comes by his office every week to "measure for drapes" — implying that this guy is gunning for Don's job. The "kid" Don is talking about is junior accounts man Peter Campbell. Fans really enjoy talking about Pete. You may recall from chapter 1 the collection of fan-created Internet memes based on this character known as Pete Campbell's Bitchface: these images showcase Pete's boyish tantrums. Fans relish talking about his shortcomings and spoiled-brat behavior. To us, Pete represents a man who does not really know how to be a man and thus reaches out to Don as a masculine role model, especially in early seasons. Fan evaluations of Pete focus primarily on his admiration of Don and attempts to emulate him and on the childishness of Pete's attitudes and behaviors.

Most of us think that the other male characters on *Mad Men* are men already, even though they aren't necessarily "good" men. Not Pete. Fans label Pete's obvious idolization of Don as one indicator of boyhood. In fact, in the Colbert interview we mentioned earlier, Matthew Weiner indicated that Pete was the man that he wanted to be when he was in high school. In that case, perhaps it isn't surprising that Pete is an underdeveloped man.

Just as a young Weiner admired guys like Pete, Pete admires Don. When Pete fails to earn Don's admiration, he tends to whine and pout. In fact, he's often socially awkward in his interactions with other men, as one fan observed: "[Other] men DO make Pete uncomfortable because he is an eternal boy in a world of men."

"I re-watched the whole series pretty recently," another viewer reflected, "and this is especially apparent in the earlier seasons: As a viewer, you actually feel uncomfortable whenever Pete approaches Don (at the old Sterling Cooper) or has a conversation with him because the character [Pete] seems so intimidated." But Pete's admiration diminishes when he learns more about Don: "The dynamic kind of changes when he finds out Don Draper is actually Dick Whitman."

Just as some fans blame Don's mother for his problems, many think Pete's need for a role model stems from his poor relationship with his father, as well as the limits of his upper-class upbringing. In the season five episode "Signal 30," fans noticed that Pete continues to measure himself against Don even outside of work: "Remember Don fixing the pipe and the way Pete looked on? Pete isn't that kind of man (as a result of being born with a silver spoon in his mouth), and in the company of men like Don or Roger, men who've been to war and can fix things, he feels insecure." This comment explains why Pete finds Don worth emulating, as well as why he appears awkward during interactions with his idol.

Another fan described this event as a metaphor for Pete's lack of the skill set associated with the male ideal in the 1960s: "When Don fixes the sink and tells Pete what was wrong [with Pete's earlier attempt to fix it], Pete comments, 'But it fixed the drip.' Don replies, 'That was just a happy coincidence' or something. . . . I think that was a pretty meaningful comment. For Pete, what originally appears as success due to his own efforts and foresight is often just mere coincidence and not all that attributable to his own work or knowledge."

In addition to comparing Pete with role model Don, fans also enjoy comparing him to our golden boy, Ken Cosgrove. For fans, the contrast between Ken's decency and Pete's indecency makes for great entertainment. When it comes to outright jealousy and challenges directed at Ken, we get to see Pete behaving badly. And much as fans are gratified by Betty's bad behavior, we love to experience through our screens what it would be like to throw a fit when things don't go our way, without having to suffer the consequences of the real world.

In season four's "Waldorf Stories," Ken is brought back to the recently formed SCDP after an absence due to the British takeover of the original firm. Ken and Pete are played directly against each other, with Pete asserting his power as a silent partner over the other man, refusing to agree to hire him unless Ken acknowledges Pete's power. Fans commented on Ken's amusement at Pete's latest power play, as well as his ability to deflect the competitive challenge that is often embedded in male representations: "I found the scene with Pete to reveal how childish he still is. He obviously is still quite insecure, which is why he makes this showy (and to me, ridiculous looking display) complete with the prop of the conference room, and the mock-casual 'I own this room' pose with his hands behind his head (which does not look natural at all because he is trying SO hard!)." Another fan adds, "I'm guessing that Ken, while nodding, was secretly laughing inside. I thought the scene also revealed that Ken is, (again?) the bigger person. Playing along with Pete and throwing him a bone — but comfortable with his position in a way Pete never is, no matter what his title, given his overall insecurity."

Pete's personality clashes and competitive antics can be painful for some of us to watch, especially if we, or someone we know, shares those characteristics. However, fans are also excited when Pete gets wound up because they know that his verbal and often physical displays will result in comedy. Here a fan deciphers why a miserable Pete is the most fun for him (and us!) to watch: "I think Cosgrove's secret is that he's relaxed and happy. I've started thinking of him as 'the most happy fella.' Pete, by contrast, is wound quite tight and I think it leaks through despite his being jovial with clients." This writer concludes, "In any case, Pete can't end up on top because his key character traits are ambition and dissatisfaction. He's far funnier when he's down a peg and fuming."

One of the most satisfying scenes for fans (including us) is, in fact, an expression of traditional masculinity. During a partner's meeting, Pete reveals to Lane that he has taken over major client Jaguar from Lane. Pete also tells his rival that the client implied that Lane was homosexual. Since fans also know that Lane is suffering personal financial issues, Pete's move seems like the culmination of challenges to Lane's masculinity.

Pete's aggression is too much for Lane, who demands a fight. Here, one fan describes the punch seen round the world as well as in the still image in figure 19: "In terms of issues of masculinity, the fight is really set off when

Figure 19. Pete Campbell's ongoing criticisms of firm copartner Lane Pryce, including remarks about Lane's sexuality, culminate in fisticuffs between the two. Lane punches Pete in the face while other partners Bert, Roger, and Don gleefully watch. Later, Joan Harris reassures Lane that everyone has wanted to punch Pete at some point (screen capture from season five, episode five, "Signal 30").

Pete . . . tells Lane that Lane's new friend thinks he's a 'homo.' Then, when Lane is the victor in the fight, he uses his adrenaline and new-found masculinity to be just like the other boys by trying to get a little office romance going [with Joan]."

After the fight Lane tries to kiss Joan, continuing on his "high" from restoring his masculinity. Like the other men in the office, Lane sees Joan as a prize. But, this fan observes, "after Joan opens the door [to keep further sexual advances at bay] and Lane apologizes, she plays dumb and asks him why he's apologizing as everyone has wanted to punch Pete in the face." Even Joan felt good about Pete getting taken down a peg!

Joan's point to Lane is really a point to the viewers. Fans were just as tired of Pete's whining and putdowns as Lane was; thus the gratification felt by fans was intense and widespread. Pete's physical embodiment of his emotional state is once more comedy gold for fans. The event resulted in many video compilations and fan art celebrating Pete getting punched right in his "Bitchface." This scene is a top fan favorite across the series.

Since neither Lane nor Pete is the alpha man, it makes sense that Lane chooses Pete to re-establish a pecking order among the male partners: "Continuing on this thread of masculinity—notice how Lane feels less of a man, and could only do so when he punched the one man in the office he could take on." In this fan's view Pete's position as an accounts man, in contrast to Lane's role as accountant, serves as another blow to Lane's abilities: "Lane could not close the deal with Jaguar, reducing him again to just a man who balances the books, as opposed to having that special human touch that would make him an accounts man."

Though fighting is a traditionally masculine behavior, fans don't necessarily approve of the way it restores the traditional pecking order. Instead, we experience intense emotional gratification in seeing Pete—often a bully—taken down a notch and finally held accountable for his foul actions. In fact, there is hardly a character we haven't seen Pete put down (his secretary, Peggy, Lane), manipulate (Ken, Trudy), or try to blackmail (Don). For us, Lane is the vehicle by which we can picture ourselves taking down a bully. Much like the scene with Betty shooting the neighbor's pigeons, or Joan smashing a vase over the head of her rapist husband, we get to vicariously experience the thrill of taking charge and balancing the scales of justice when Lane puts his fists up. The experience is sweeter because Pete is a character we have seen in action up close, and it is easy for us to rally against him.

In order to become more "manly," Pete attempts to achieve power by manipulation and competitive behavior, even though these behaviors do not always result in the desired outcomes. Moreover, in the fans' eyes he's a boy who is trying to become more like the men around him, even when they are not perfect examples of good men themselves. In fact, ironically, the role models he identifies and his behaviors mean that fans continue to judge him as a child who has never grown up.

Other Masculine Behaviors

In addition to discussing individual characters, fans also see overall messages about masculinity embedded in the behavior of both main and minor male characters on the show. Some fans believe these behaviors are inherently male and persist across generations, while others attribute them to the 1960s atmosphere, without a clear majority favoring either view. Regardless of whether they blame the historical period, many fans identify risky behavior, excessive consumption, stunted emotional capacities, heterosexual prowess, social stodginess, and financial responsibilities as key elements of manhood on *Mad Men*.

We've seen the examples of emotional stuntedness earlier in fans' interpretations of both Don and Pete. Both these characters and Roger Sterling also engage in heterosexual relationships to demonstrate their sexual prowess in front of other men — proving their worth to each other by obtaining and showing off desirable women. One fan addresses how Roger's scene with the twin actresses — as his sexual conquests — plays out as both a stereotypical fantasy and a train wreck: "I'm pretty sure Roger with the twins was supposed to be pathetic. . . . You could see how someone like Roger would think it would be an awesome moment in his head (and hell, on another show it might have been) and it just comes out all wrong." For this fan Matthew Weiner succeeds in revealing the very real problems caused by one aspect of the traditional masculine ideal.

In addition to warped sexual and emotional behaviors, fans frequently list excessive drinking, smoking, and drug use as associated with masculinity on the show. "Hijinks" and related juvenile or dangerous behaviors are tickets to enter the "boys club." One instance of these activities is the aforementioned fisticuffs between Lane and Pete; another is a confrontation between a very drunk Herman "Duck" Phillips (one-time SC employee, who is later employed at a rival firm, and occasional flame of Peggy's) and Don. Such acts of "manhood" display the characters' physical strength — a key masculine trait.

One fan notices that in many cases our main character, Don, declines to engage in instances of debauchery, at least on a group level: "The episode 'The Crash' opens . . . with the hijinks of the GM execs who are such sadistic risk-takers (they are more like Enron execs than any GM execs I can think of) that they nearly kill Ken with their 'joy ride.'" But Don declines to join them: "That is the kind of masculine world that Don understandably keeps at bay — that is, the kind of world that has alienated him from male companionship, which he never seeks for its own sake."

It is interesting that fans think Don is above such displays of masculinity as a team effort, but not one-on-one. For example, they mention that Don tricks Roger — getting him drunk and causing him to throw up in front of a client — after Roger made a pass at Betty in season one, episode seven, "Red in the Face."

Matthew Weiner has said that Don is a reflection of traditional masculinity and the conflicting ideas that come with figuring out how to be a man. Fans readily categorize, analyze, and understand the facets of manhood on *Mad Men* from the perspectives of specific characters. They agree with Weiner that Don is conflicted, and they take the position that all of the male characters would be better men and better people if they were more like Ken Cosgrove. This character seems to some viewers to be the only real grown-up, while others see him as a counterimage to a prefeminist Don.

The arguments for both these views are strong. Ken's refusal to compete with a jealous Pete and his reluctance to continue on the Chevy account when his life is jeopardized are sound decisions by a fully functioning adult. His supportive and mutually beneficial work relationship with Peggy and his unwavering refusal to exploit his wife's connections in order to advance his career demonstrate feminist principles of recognizing women's worth and engaging in egalitarian relationships.

But Ken is the exception, not the rule. With all the cringe-inducing situations we see Don, Pete, and Roger get into in order to assert their masculinity, it is pretty clear that *Mad Men* as a whole does not celebrate these behaviors. Instead, the emotional and even physical discomfort that viewers experience while watching serves as a reminder that such behavior was not only uncomfortable in the past and that it still doesn't work for men today. Certainly *Mad Men* has played a role in provoking fan discussions about the ongoing evolution of masculinity and the erosion of the hard line between gender roles.

As we mentioned in the previous chapter, just because a behavior is shown on a show doesn't mean that the program is celebrating it. We wish that some of the potential fans who were turned off by *Mad Men* because they thought the show itself was sexist would give it another try. If you hang in there, you'll see there's something subtler and more important going on in a world that purposefully appears to be something it's not. Appearances are not always what they seem to be: some argue that this is a main theme of the show that plays itself out on many levels.

And actually, that's one of the approaches of *Mad Men* that we like — the ability that the new media convergence culture affords us to deliver a complex story for a savvy audience that doesn't need messages to hit them over the head. This is an audience that can savor a show like a fine wine, waiting for all the subtlety of its mysteries to be revealed. In the first half of season seven, Don is back at work, Peggy is his boss, and we are on the edge of our seats.

CHAPTER SEVEN

Let's Get It On: Love and Sex on *Mad Men*

How could we talk about *Mad Men* without talking about sex? It was the sixties, and "Make love not war" was the slogan. Sterling Cooper was a hotbed of sex. The office "girls" were regular conquests of the ad men, who leered and prowled around them like lions with a piece of meat. Pete and Peggy's short-lived affair resulted in pregnancy. Joan had an ongoing affair with Roger, also resulting in a lovechild. Betty had sex with a stranger in the bathroom of a bar. And, of course, Don slept with nearly every woman who crossed his path.

But it's Don himself who insists that there's much more to it than sex. When the young Peggy says, "Sex sells," Don replies, "Says who? Just so you know, the people who talk that way think that monkeys can do this. They take all this monkey crap and just stick it in a briefcase completely unaware that their success depends on something more than their shoeshine. *You* are the product. You—*feeling* something. That's what sells. Not them. Not sex. They can't do what we do, and they hate us for it" (season two, episode three, "The Benefactor"). He means advertising, but as the fans know his insight applies to life too. As one of them wrote, "When it comes to the central characters it's never about the sex; it's always about their emotional needs."

Indeed, in *Mad Men* sexual relationships are a critical life force influencing almost every story line in the show. *Mad Men* creator, Matthew Weiner, in an AMC video interview, calls the show "psychological storytelling," where the psychological texture is both internal and symbolic. He says, "When you see sex on the show it is about how we see ourselves, how we are seen by other people, all the other trappings of society sort of disappear for a moment and a rule is broken." It is through acts of sex that we see the characters of *Mad Men* explore their lives, their connections, their identity, and their self-esteem.

There is what psychologists call an "appetitive/aversive" dichotomy in the way that sex is portrayed on *Mad Men*. On the one hand, there are beautiful people and sexy scenes. On the other hand, there are difficult life events that put sexuality in a harsh light in the show. When fans talk sex, they frequently become more serious and turn to examining relationships. A fan, when describing Don, pragmatically states, "His affairs are always about giving him power that he doesn't otherwise feel."

Many condemn Don for his debauchery. Some also condemn him for marrying Megan — at least for the way he did it (proposing seemingly out of the blue and abruptly ending his relationship with Dr. Faye Miller). Fans also differentiate between meaningless sex and meaningful bonds. For instance, they know that Ted is crossing a moral boundary when he falls in love and sleeps with Peggy. But ultimately, they want the relationship between Peggy and Ted to happen because it represents a genuine affection and a bonding of equals. Generally, fans long for healthy, fulfilling relationships for the characters, wishing they would get it right. Where is the healthy sex? Can the characters ever have sex with the "right person" for the "right reasons"?

Housewives and Working Girls

Let's turn our attention to the subject of sex and gender roles — specifically the contrast between the working man in Manhattan and the stay-at-home mom in the 'burbs. Consider all the steamy sex in the city going on against the backdrop of the suburban housewife spending hours and hours at home, often frustrated, raising a family almost by herself, spending long hours waiting for her husband to return home from work.

Bored to tears at the house, Betty spends some of her time fantasizing about a door-to-door salesman and the erotic potential of the washing machine. What a juxtaposition of the image of the wife at home — her life as it was and how she sometimes wished it would be, expressed through sexual longing. Contrast Betty's domestic cage with Peggy, sitting in a hotel room in nothing but her bra and panties at first — and then getting naked, trying to get a reluctant Stan to engage with the current ad campaign instead of his *Playboy*.

Figure 20. Demonstrating a female can wield both power and sexuality, Peggy sits naked working with Stan in the Waldorf stories. What a contrast to suburban housewife Betty (screen capture from season four, episode six, "Waldorf Stories").

A fan discusses the challenges and complexity of these issues by talking about how difficult it is for Peggy to be accepted in her role as a working girl separate from her sexual identity, saying, "Men who you didn't want to sleep with constantly accused you of being repressed, out of touch with your sexuality, not being liberated enough—and there was enough 'liberation' in the air (the *Playboy* pix) that such guys could point to. This guy refused to deal with Peggy on a professional level, harping instead on her supposed 'repression.' By calling his bluff on how liberated he was, Peggy finally got out of him what she wanted: some sketches. I thought it was a really accurate depiction of the kind of nonsense women had to put up with all the time to be taken seriously in a business—and, I don't think the deadline would have made any difference. He would have continued to jerk her around by not focusing on the task at hand forever if she hadn't taken charge of the situation."

The contrast between Betty and Peggy in those days makes Peggy's life look so much more powerful, sexy, and appealing. This raises the larger issue of married women and sex. This particular example (Betty on the washing machine and Peggy naked writing copy) blurs the line between whether we're talking primarily about sex and sexiness or about stay-at-home moms versus working girls and the cultural mores surrounding women's sexuality for housewives versus workers. And, an even larger issue — which, if any, of these women is fulfilled in these circumstances?

Fans also struggle with whether or not the writers truly capture the essence of women's experience in the sixties. One fan wrote, "While the writers show great complexity in their development of working women at a turning point, they do not seem to know what to do about motherhood. If *Mad Men* has a weakness at all, I think it's in its seeming inability to get past the Madonna/ whore dichotomy."

Don Draper

Married twice and divorced once (or thrice and twice if you count Anna Draper), protagonist Don Draper is also the most visible sexually active character on *Mad Men*. We watch him leave many women brokenhearted as a result of everything from casual dalliances to rather intense coupling (including two of those marriages), and we speculate on whether he is happy, in love, or even aware of what he is doing. Poor Don never seems to be able to get it right. Viewers lament, "Don usually leaves his mistresses when 'real life' gets in the way. He stopped sleeping with Sally's teacher once Betty discovered his past, Sylvia's over once Sally catches them, and once he finds out Bobbie's heard about him from other woman, same deal. Once the fantasy is interrupted, he has no interest."

As a result, fans find it necessary to keep a running list of his conquests. "I couldn't help but audibly groan every time Don was alone with a pretty woman last season, like 'yup, he'll probably do her . . . fantastic,'" complains one fan, speaking for many viewers. Though Don's sexual conquests are too numerous (and sometimes too obscure) to list, a selection of his sexual partners include his first/second wife, now Betty Francis, who married Henry, a Rockefeller aide; his second/third wife, Megan Draper, an aspiring actress, previously a receptionist and copywriter at Sterling Cooper; Midge Daniels, an artist living in Greenwich Village and Don's early creative muse; Rachel Menken, client and head of a family department store (some fans think Don loved her); Bobbie Barrett, the wife of Utz Chip, a comedian and ad talent, with whom the sex starts to get violent; Sally Draper's third-grade teacher, Susanne Farrell; Dr. Faye Miller, a psychologist consulting for the agency; Sylvia Rosen, the neighbor living one floor below Megan and Don; and a variety of flight attendants, prostitutes, office secretaries, and wealthy Palm Springs socialites.

Fans wrestle with why Don has all these affairs and what they mean. Troubled by the contradictions of Don's sex life, a fan writes, "The irony of Don's affair choice: while married to Betty, a housewife, Don chose affairs with independent or professional women. Now that he's married to an 'independent' woman, on her way to a successful career [that's Megan], he is having an affair with a housewife who welcomes an 'allowance' from him (i.e., the cookie jar money) [Sylvia]."

Given Don's proclivity for casual liaisons, viewers can't help but take note of three important women he doesn't sleep with: Peggy Olson, his protégée and the character that *Mad Men* creator Matthew Weiner calls Don's mirror. Nor does he have sex with Joan Holloway, the office manager and femme fatale who later becomes a partner in the firm, or Anna Draper, the wife of the real Don Draper (who died in the Korean War and whose name and life Dick Whitman assumed). So why doesn't Don sleep with these three women?

They all appear to be important female figures in his life, and he seems to care deeply for them. It is such a contrast to his normal modus operandi. A fan speculates, "Anna, Peggy and Joan are the three woman he truly cares for. No surprise that he never had sex with them. Difficult childhoods make for difficult adulthoods. Look at the people around you. I am always in Don's corner, he represents hope for all of us just trying to get through the day." Another fan argues, "Another easy thing for viewers to swallow—Don has a different relationship with Joan and Peggy (and to a lesser extent, Faye) because they are in his world at every level and every day. He can physically leave his wife and his mistresses in their 'proper' compartments, but Peggy and Joan defy this classification, which forces him to see them as real people."

With Anna, fans say that she knows his secret and so he doesn't have to hide behind the facade of the self-confident sexual conqueror. Viewers carefully consider Don's emotional state in his relationships with women: "I feel like the only time in the show Don ever seemed *truly* happy was when he was with Anna. A sexless relationship/friendship in which he got to be Dick Whitman." Fans talk about how sex might be the offending factor: once engaged, respect is lost and emotions closed. Don obviously values his relationship with Anna. Could it be because he does not have sex with Anna? He is both more and less vulnerable with her. Less vulnerable because he does not need to fear she will discover the truth about him (she already knows). Yet he is more vulnerable because he no longer can hide behind the veneer of Don Draper. He is Dick Whitman, raw and unprotected.

Joan, on the other hand, garners Don's respect in a different way. Her strength and independence are juxtaposed with her feminine charm. In season five, episode ten, "Christmas Waltz," Don rescues Joan during the divorce papers incident by taking her out of the office for the day and test-driving a Jaguar. A fan talks about the Jaguar day, saying, "The scenes between Don and Joan were just wonderful. Two people who have a common understanding." He doesn't want her to sleep with Herb Rennet to secure the Jaguar account (season five, episode eleven, "The Other Woman") and goes to her to stop her from doing so (albeit too late, she sleeps with Herb to secure a partnership at SCDP). One fan describes the relationship as "Don likes and respects Joan, and Don isn't very attracted to women he likes and respects. His challenge has always been to find someone who's somewhere in between a Peggy and a Betty, and then not to get scared and fuck it all up. But that person's not Joan. She's a lot closer to Peggy in Don's mind."

Peggy is often thought to be a female Don. Fans and Matthew Weiner alike see Peggy as Don's reflection and believe that we need both characters to understand either. As we watch Don crumble physically and emotionally and his productivity at work begin to decline, Peggy grows creatively and becomes increasingly successful. The fans notice that the camera always shows Don looking backward and Peggy looking forward. Does Don represent the past and Peggy the future? Is the only way for Peggy to flourish for Don to fall? A fan wisely observes, "Obviously, this is *Mad Men* and there will always be more questions than answers."

Sex and Power

Fans often see Don's sexual escapades as his attempt to establish a power dynamic in which he controls the other person. The idea of sex as power struggle is never more evident than in the relationship between Don and Betty. A big shift in their dynamic happens when Betty confronts Don about having an affair (with Bobbie Barrett) in the second season, episode eight, "A Night to Remember." Accustomed to using her sexuality to control and influence men (not unlike Don with women), Betty was left angry and helpless.

Fans sympathize with Betty's hopelessness when in the season two finale, "Meditations in an Emergency," she realizes she has to remain with an unfaithful Don (she finds out she is pregnant). A viewer wonders what resolve Betty could possibly have under the burden of her situation given that time period (the sixties), stating, "Whatever thing was aspirational about Betty, it's been constantly crushed by her environment, and most of all by her husband."

After seeing her doctor, who denies her an abortion, a determined Betty leaves the kids with Don at his hotel—where she has him cooling his heels after his confession of cheating—and seeks to even the score. Set on the eve of the Cuban missile crisis, Betty attracts a handsome stranger in a bar. He buys her a drink and later they sneak into the back office to have sex. Yes, she still has it. She is attractive, and she can stir desire in men. She might not be able to control Don, but she still has her sexual power. And given her social environment she has no choice, at least in her mind, but to remain married to Don and have the baby. For the time being, the power, or at least the perception of power, remains with Don.

But many seasons later Betty takes the opportunity to leverage her sexual power. Divorced and both married to other people, Don and Betty hook up again for a brief affair while visiting their son Bobbie at his summer camp (season six, episode nine, "The Better Half"). Fans pointed out that sleeping with Don didn't have much to do with love for Betty but was rather a celebration of using her body again, "a rediscovered source of pride." Alone for the weekend without their current spouses, Don and Betty had sex, and the power equation changed in her favor. A viewer described, "I read into the Don/Betty scene that it was about shifting the balance. When Betty looked over at him in the restaurant the next morning the look said she had the power now."

And marriage isn't the only kind of sexual relationship in which Don and his partner play power games. In season two Don and Bobbie Barrett's relationship is very much about power, and they play with it quite a bit, actually enjoying the fluidity as it shifts back and forth. One fan captures the essence of Don and Bobbie's sex/power dynamic: "Bobbie uses sex against Don and he flips it to being the one in charge of her. It is a turn on for Bobbie that he pulls the power on her." At one point the sex turns violent when Don finds out that Bobbie has been talking to others about their affair, certainly a no-no for tight-lipped, self-contained Don, and well, he has a wife and all. He ties her to the bed with his belt, and the sex gets even fiercer in intensity and power.

The deeper Don dives into, or should we say gets overcome by, the narcotic addiction of sex as power, the more manipulative he becomes. A good example is Don's affair with his neighbor Sylvia, who is married to a man Don appears to like, maybe even admire (season six). Fans try to make sense of this relationship. One viewer said, "Don Draper, the man you love to hate. Seducing the wife of a man he clearly admires and respects is a new low, even for Don. I'm trying to figure out if he's doing it because he wants to, even if only Sylvia and he know about the affair, be able to hold it over her husband's head; if now Don sees himself as the superior male. Or if he really hates Arnold, and this is his way of stabbing the esteemed doctor in the back. Whatever. I hate to think of the look on Arnold's face when the truth is revealed and he realizes he was betrayed by a man he liked."

Almost in the same league but nowhere near as suave and certainly perceived as much more degenerate, Pete Campbell also wields power through his sexual encounters. Fans wax less romantic about Pete's affair, saying he "loves the power of being able to sleep around on his wife" and uses sex and dominance more out of boredom than control. As one fan puts it, "Pete's affairs are less a product of the times and society (although there is still that element of entitledness) and more about his general disenchantment: his parents and his heritage fail him, his wife fails him, his job fails him, and most of all he fails himself. He wants to feel empowered when his coworkers don't respect him (aside from his name), his wife walks all over him, and his parents essentially hate him. His affairs are always about giving him power that he doesn't otherwise feel."

He coerced Peggy, the new office girl, into having sex to validate his power (pilot episode). One fan understood his perspective on the event this way: "I always took it as Peggy just having fun and enjoying being a young girl, which is who she is. She's single, independent, and sexy, so naturally, Pete Campbell is threatened by that and has to ruin the experience for her. He wants to 'own' her, like the woman in the fantasy he told her about in the previous episode. He wants to hunt for a submissive creature, and this is her acting completely opposite that type."

Calling Joan both a survivor and a whore, fans struggle with how to justify her actions. Should they respect her or hate her? She is raped by her fiancé in her boss's office (season two, episode twelve). She is whistled at, objectified, and sexually harassed by her coworkers. She weaves office-manager magic in making the office staff function seamlessly and efficiently. She is raising her child as a single parent — all while being underpaid compared to her male colleagues and still keeping a relatively upbeat approach. And then Joan agrees to have sex with a Jaguar client to secure the automobile account and to land a partnership in the firm (season five, episode eleven). Brilliant, intelligent, strategic, whorish — that's our Joan.

Fans get fired up in the debate: Is she or isn't she a prostitute? Some defend her, comparing her actions to those of her male colleagues and men in general. For example, it wouldn't be considered an issue if one of the men from the office slept with an unattractive female client to land an account, and if he did, we certainly wouldn't call him a prostitute. Think Don with Rachel Menken, the department store owner, or Bobbie Barrett, wife and agent of Utz ad talent. One fan empathizes with Joan, saying, "Joan does feel shame and disgust for the act, and I teared up when she unzipped her dress, but was it an act of prostitution? Don't know, which is why I thought it was such a brilliant episode. She's not coming at the act from a position of power, but she's not powerless. Will her new partners have respect for her guts, never quite respect her because of how she got there, some combination thereof?"

"Her sexual act doesn't have to be read as morally corrupt. Nor does her business decision define her or cement her identity as 'prostitute,'" another fan states, supporting Joan's decision to use her sexuality strategically, like almost every other character on *Mad Men*.

But some of the fans cannot get past Joan's actions, referencing her sexual history as, among other things, Roger's mistress. These fans are stunned by her behavior and chastise her, claiming she "used her sexuality to get ahead, she was no better than a prostitute to begin with, and, therefore, the Jaguar deal was, well, no big deal."

Finally, some fans label Joan as a survivor and a product of her times. She had been raised to wait for the white knight to take care of her, put her on a pedestal. And yet she didn't just stand there on a pedestal. Instead, she showed that she had "a bit of Scarlett O'Hara streak to her — she's a survivor and will do what she needs to do to make it."

Affairs and the Business of Marriage

Despite the lingering double standard, fans struggle as they try to make meaning of why the characters on *Mad Men* — male and female — are having affairs. What is it that makes them seek sex outside their marriages and do so prolifically? Is it addiction, control, or trying to find their mother? What is the motivation? Why the lies? These are the questions we ask, not so that we can understand fictional characters whose motives are ultimately determined by writers but so that we can understand life. Show creator Matthew Weiner, in an AMC video review of season four, suggests that one of the reasons we as viewers are drawn into watching all the sex on *Mad Men* is so we can live vicariously through the characters, seeing through the character's eyes what it is like. We get to visit our deepest, darkest fantasies. In essence, we get to try it on for size and cheat without repercussions. Or as Bobbie Barrett says to Don in season one, episode five, about their affair, "I like being bad then going home and being good."

Even if Pete Campbell is fictional, people who share his common traits and experiences do exist. And that's why it's important to understand Pete. We share the belief that, in addition to understanding others, thinking about each character also helps us understand ourselves better. We wouldn't like to admit it, but sometimes maybe we have a little bit of Pete or a little bit of Don in us. We ask ourselves why they do what they do and whether we might do something similar, given similar opportunities or circumstances.

Thus we look for motives that make the characters' behaviors understandable. As one fan wrote, "Unlike Pete, who's an asshole who cheats because he thinks it makes him powerful, I think Don cheats because it's compulsive and it's ultimately really sad." But another fan countered, "What about Pete and Peggy and their BABY!!! . . . I think the saddest [affair] is Pete and Peggy, mostly for her naive expectations and the eventual baby." In fact, "sad" is how fans describe most of the affairs that occur during the show: Ted's no-win situation when he got involved with Peggy despite being married, Don's one-night stand with a secretary, and Pete's neglect of Peggy when she tries to flirt with him publicly.

The sexual encounter between Don and his secretary Allison in season four, episode two, "Christmas Comes But Once a Year," particularly pulled on the fans' heartstrings, who sensed the incredible pain Allison must be experiencing. One fan lamented, "Amongst the saddest affairs on *Mad Men* was the one between Don and his secretary, Allison who basically got used and spit out and then was expected to show up to work every day as if nothing happened. She finally had to resign. I felt so bad for that poor girl, who thought for a moment that her luck was changing that Don noticed her then so a swift kick in the stomach when he completely abandoned her."

The ultimate sadness, though, seems to come from watching Don sink deeper and deeper into the abyss with his serial affairs. His affairs seem empty and unenjoyable, and he pursues them almost like a drug addict who has to maintain a certain level just to keep from going through withdrawal. One fan explained it this way: "His cheating is connected with his inability to stay content in life. He'll be happy with his wife for a while, until he needs more happiness, leading him to find a mistress, who will keep him happy until he needs more happiness."

Eventually he does get caught — Betty realizes he's been unfaithful to her. Early in the series (season 1, episode 13) she had talked about marital fidelity, saying, "Still, I can't help but think that I'd be happy if my husband was faithful to me." But realizing there is something amiss, she complains, "The way he makes love—sometimes it's what I want and sometimes, it's obviously what someone else wants." Fans observe Don taking advantage of Betty's naïveté and thinking of her as someone he could control—sex as power again.

And yet again fans still forgive him and excuse his behavior, saying he is looking for his mother in other women. For fans Don is a special case: "He's grown up in a whorehouse, the son of a whore, so he's been witness to men who cheat on their wives. He's fled from that life, but by lying and cheating. He discovers he has a gift for selling things to people, to creating a lie that convinces people to want what they don't have, to be happy. And he lives that lie, he's always lived that lie—men who want the whore they don't have at home, a man who wants another man's life. So for him, those women are what he can't or shouldn't have, they're the lie he's convinced himself he needs to be happy. But he never truly is, and so he moves on."

Despite the debate (prostitution or power play) over Joan's decision to have sex with the Jaguar dealer (season five, episode eleven), fans readily excuse her other sexual relationships. They consider Joan's brief encounter with Roger (the one that resulted in a child while she was still married to Greg) redeemable, claiming Greg was a bad human and, as Roger said, "it was a moment" (season four, episode nine). Fans also were fairly kind to Roger, considering his long list of affairs and rather tawdry sex, saying, "Wow, with all of his dalliances, he's had a wide variety of motivations. Ultimately, though, he's used to getting what he wants, and this often includes extra-marital lovers." The surprising fan light-heartedness reflects Roger's own attitude. As he says in the first season, "I guess what I'm saying is at some point we've all parked in the wrong garage" (season one, episode seven). Clearly, the male characters benefit from the double standard of the times—they could have sex without consequences, while women could not.

Does love factor into all the sex happening on *Mad Men*? Fans tend to agree that the only real love they see from Don is toward his children and possibly Anna. They disagree about whether Don ever loves his wives Betty and Megan, debating both sides. We know he is cynical about love; in the third season, episode two, "Love Among the Ruins," he says, "By love you mean big lightning bolts to the heart, where you can't eat and you can't work, and you just run off and get married and make babies. The reason you haven't felt it is because it doesn't exist. What you call love was invented by guys like me . . . to sell nylons." But at least some of the women do seem to feel genuine love. In season six, episode nine, "The Better Half," Betty tells Don, "That poor girl [Megan]. She doesn't know that loving you is the worst way to get to you."

Fans recognize that the differences in the ways that men and women experience sex and love in the show reflect the double standard prevalent during the 1960s. Husbands were free to have sex when and where they wanted it, and yet conversely they expected their wives to be sexually faithful to them. In one instance Don was upset and jealous when Megan kissed a man during a scene in a soap opera—without apparently feeling bad about his own constant philandering. One *Mad Men* fan commented, "I think a lot of them [the show's characters] are probably influenced by the people around them as it's the sort of male culture that existed back then; where married guys did what they wanted and expected to get away with it because they were generally the dominant gender."

Discussing the show's second season, Weiner himself cast marriage as a strategic negotiation: "It is complicated because there are things you want, loyalties being tested." And both male and female characters understand it that way. Betty tells Don they make a great team. She brings up her sexuality in reference to holding up her end of the marital bargain: "As far as I'm concerned, as long as men look at me that way, I'm earning my keep." And in season two, episode five, Roger alludes in his comical, pejorative Roger way to the business of marriage and sex, saying, "I'll tell you the same thing I told my daughter: if you put a penny in a jar every time you make love in the first year of marriage, and then you take a penny out of the jar every time you make love in the second year, you know what you have?"

The business quality of marriages on *Mad Men* brings together all the themes of love and control, marital sex and infidelity to explain why some marriages persist while others fail. Oddly, as dysfunctional as Pete is as a character, his marriage is often cited by the fans as the best one on *Mad Men* because wife Trudy makes it work—at least on the surface. Yes, viewers know the reality is that their marriage is a complete and utter mess. But the appearance of their marriage to other people seems to matter more. As one fan wrote, "Trudy's anger stemmed not from the fact of Pete's adultery but from his sloppiness, cheating with a woman from the same block. She had allowed the New York apartment to keep his infidelities out of sight and out of mind. But she refuses 'to be a failure,' as she thinks she would be after a divorce, so the new arrangement requires Pete to stay away except when she calls him in for appearance's sake. Believe her when she says she would destroy him—under her innocent veneer, she knows full well that she holds the social and economic power in their relationship and comes from a family with much more real-world power than Pete's, which is little more than the fading Dyckman name." The business of marriage is a strong business that does not necessarily need to include sex to remain viable.

Identity

The relationship between sex and selfhood is also challenged by the show's setting—an advertising agency. The advertisements that the show's characters create often misidentify or skew sexuality precisely in order to sell. For example, in season two, episode six, "Maidenform," the creative team is busy at work creating a Maidenform bra ad campaign. The hook: women were cast as either a Marilyn or a Jackie (as in Marilyn Monroe or Jacqueline Kennedy Onassis), leaving women very little leeway to feel sexy and connected to their sexuality if they did not identify with either.

Is Joan really a Marilyn, and if so, what would that mean? Young Sally knows. Sitting in Don's office being watched by Joan, she says, "You've got big ones. My mommy has big ones. When I grow up, I'm gonna have big ones too" (season two, episode four). As a fan states, "You know that kid is going to have an interesting life" because of the gender roles and sexual promiscuity she sees all around her. Clearly she already knows that her body will be her most important asset. Fans talk about all the sexual encounters Sally happens upon (Roger receiving oral sex from Megan's mother in the "At the Codfish Ball" episode or Don having sex with neighbor Sylvia in the episode "Favors"). One fan comments that "many of her scenes make me wince because the adults response—not Sally's behavior—is what we now know is completely inappropriate." How is this kid ever going to have a healthy sex life?

Mad Men also takes on other sexual taboos. For instance, there are several

Figure 21. The odd childhood sexuality of Glen's creepiness with Betty when later in the series he ends up being important to Sally. Here we see Glen and Betty on the couch together before Glen tries to put the moves on Betty (hold her hand) (screen capture from season one, episode four, "New Amsterdam").

story lines that involve childhood sexuality. There is a lot of love for Sally among the fans in general. And this is no less true when she is "caught" masturbating. Fans feel for Sally and want her to grow up to develop a healthy sexuality. They are not happy with Betty for the way she treats Sally during the "Chrysanthemum and the Sword" episode in season four. Fans see Betty's reaction as demonstrating more concern for her image and reputation than the welfare of her children. One fan stated, "Betty is fundamentally incapable of seeing her children as human beings, instead they are external representations of her" and noted that she perceived Sally's behavior as a personal insult. Other fans see Betty's actions toward Sally as unraveling, as having an Electra complex, a bitter demonstration of jealousy and concern for what others will think more than anything else. It is all about the image; Betty is ashamed with Sally and what people will think. A fan asks, "Why is Betty so angry at Sally? Because she is jealous of Sally."

Then there is the rather strange story of forbidden love between, of all people, the character Glen (played by Matthew Weiner's son, Marten Holden Weiner) and Betty. Glen is a neighborhood boy and the young son of a divorced mother. He is infatuated with Betty. In season one, episode four, the "New Amsterdam" episode, when Betty babysits Glen, he asks her for a lock of her hair and purposely walks in on her in the bathroom. Fans find ways to justify Glen's creepiness as that of a lonely and sexually curious young boy, but they are a bit more unhinged at Betty's participation in the whole relationship—her holding hands with Glen when they watch television and giving him a lock of her hair. A viewer explains it as "coming as it did at a time when she was so repressed that her hands went numb from her unacknowledged anger at her husband, I see the weirdness with Glen as Betty wanting, desperately, to connect with anyone who saw her as a perfect."

Gay Characters

Amid all the rampant heterosexuality, it's worth mentioning that several of the *Mad Men* characters are gay, some more openly than others. Fans like to talk about Sal Romano, the art director. He tries to hide that he is gay and twice avoids sexual encounters with different men at the office. On the other hand, while on a business trip with Don (season three, episode one), he starts to seduce a bellhop. They get caught when the fire alarm goes off, and all end up outside the hotel in various states of undress. Not surprisingly, the alarm catches Don, too, in an embarrassing situation—it's obvious that he has been seducing a stewardess. Perhaps as a result, he isn't upset to realize that Sal is gay. One fan wrote, "Don seemed more 'surprised' than morally outraged by Sal's romp with the bellboy. Matthew Weiner shows his consummate skill and obsessive attention for period detail once again by reminding us that by the early 1960s, homosexual relations were a subject of curiosity more than anything else."

Many of the story lines around homosexuality in *Mad Men* are, as one fan called it, "frustratingly disorganized," with characters disappearing without warning. The same fan asks, "Whatever happened to Joan's closeted lesbian roommate [and] are we ever going to see Sal again?" He has been absent for half the series. Fans are upset that he hasn't returned again. They miss him. As one fan asked, "Anyone else hoping Rizzo (new 'art director'/pig) gets

Figure 22. While on a business trip to Baltimore Sal engages in an extramarital liaison. Here we see the bellman kissing Sal in the hotel room just before the fire alarm rings (screen capture from season three, episode one, "Out of Town").

the boot by Don and we see the return of lovely Sal? (I'm keeping my fingers crossed)." While small roles are given to Kurt, a creative at Sterling Cooper, and Joyce, Peggy's openly gay friend, their story lines are infrequent and brief.

While he didn't completely fill the void left by the vanishing Sal, viewers do see Bob Benson struggling with some of the classic challenges of being gay in the sixties and growing a career on Madison Avenue. In season seven, episode six, "The Strategy," Bob is shown bailing out a friend who was a victim of abuse by a homophobic NYPD officer. Fans seem to like Bob but attack his choice (or rather, should we say the show creator's choice?) of affection. For example, one fan argues, "Now if he was in love with Kenny, Don, Roger or Stan, I'd buy it, but Pete is such a whiner and pouts around the office like a big baby. What the hell does Bob see in him? Pete's a weenie. And all of Bob's lies still aren't quite explained. I hope there is more of Bob to reveal." Another fan calls out Matthew Weiner directly on his handling of *Mad Men* characters' sexuality, saying, "Dear Mr. Weiner; You've turned nearly every young, sexy guy on this show into revolting pieces of trash. Could you please keep your destructive paws off of Bob Benson? He's an adorable hottie and we'd love to have just a single hero to hang our hats on? Thanks."

Sexuality Fun and Flawed

Part of the changing times that serve as the backdrop to *Mad Men* were the changing sexual mores. Fans laugh, they sympathize, and sometimes they can hardly believe all the sexual activity taking place. And some note how much times have changed. One fan commented on whether Don Draper would survive today in his sexually charged state: "I'm laughing at all the men admiring Don Draper and wanting to be him. Try it guys! You do realize this was set in the 60s? Don Draper wouldn't survive the 2010s — he's barely surviving the 60s! You think so many young, beautiful women today would put up with his complete and utter contempt of them without at least a bit of a fight? He's completely wet, emotionally crippled, lacking in morals, cowardly, miserable as sin, and lonely. (Furthermore I always suspected him to be a bit rubbish in bed because there's never much foreplay. The women are faking it)."

Some of the sex in *Mad Men* could be described as playful and fun — the kind of tantalizing pleasure we imagine how many feel about simply seeing Joan in her sexy sixties outfits. There are moments of passion and love — delightful rolls in the hay. But then there's also the dark side — and there is plenty of darkness in the sexuality explored in *Mad Men*. Perhaps Joan herself shows us a tableau of the light, the dark, and the twisted. There are fun moments, like when she sweetly lets Lane down after he makes a rather gentlemanly pass at her on his office sofa after punching Pete Campbell (this is arguable, as even the authors of this book couldn't agree whether an uninvited kiss should be considered gentlemanly). Then there are deeply troubling scenes like the confrontation with the office employee who seems hellbent on labeling her as a whore. There's everything from the way she made it up the ladder at SCDP to a rape scene involving her own fiancé. Sexuality in Joan's life is not for the faint of heart. And the same could be said for how sexuality is treated on the entire show.

On *Mad Men* there are beautiful people and sexy scenes, and there are difficult life events that cast a harsh and hard light on sexuality. But the appearance versus the sexualized reality doesn't have to be all bad. As Roger says in the first season, episode ten, "The Long Weekend," "When God closes a door, he opens a dress."

CHAPTER EIGHT

Ad Men: For Those Who Think Young

Advertising is based on one thing: happiness. And you know what
happiness is? Happiness is the smell of a new car. It's freedom from fear.
It's a billboard on the side of the road that screams reassurance that
whatever you are doing is okay. You are okay.

— Don Draper, season one, episode one, "Smoke Gets in Your Eyes"

Like cocktails and client meetings, like Sterling and Cooper, like Don Draper
and . . . every woman he ever set his mind to bedding, *Mad Men* and advertising are forever linked. And people in advertising love *Mad Men*. By the start
of the show's second season in 2008, it had become so popular with advertising professionals that the industry publication *Advertising Age* produced a
fictional *Mad Men*–centric issue to help promote the show. That popularity
is also what catalyzed a group of fans, who were predominantly people working in advertising, to start tweeting as *Mad Men* characters — a phenomenon
we explored in chapter 4.

One of the authors of this book, Cynthia, had first-hand experience with
the effect that *Mad Men* could have within the industry. She once worked
at an advertising agency called RPA, which became abuzz when Sterling
Cooper Draper Pryce pitched Honda motorcycles in a season four episode.
RPA's major client was American Honda Motor Company, and colleagues
who were fans of the show felt an instant connection to this *Mad Men* story
line. RPA even produced a video interview with one of the firm's founders,
Gerry Rubin, in which he talked about his experience pitching to Honda as
well as his impressions of the show.

While there are a lot of television shows about cops, lawyers, and doctors
on the air, there is only one recent successful show that focuses on the inner
workings of an advertising agency — and advertising professionals appreciate
Mad Men for that. Even if the show is a period piece, it seems that many ad-

vertising men and women get a thrill out of seeing the industry they work in depicted on television. And why not? After all, people often define themselves, at least in part, by their profession, and their profession becomes an important part of their self-concept as a result. People understand this intuitively. On meeting someone new you've likely been asked what you do for a living. Or maybe you've done the asking. The answer to the question helps people get to know each other a little better. In other words, our occupation says something about who we are.

For advertising professionals, then, *Mad Men* is highly self-relevant, because its focus on their industry gives them something personal to connect to. And because of their personal connection, fans of *Mad Men* who work in advertising and related fields, like marketing and public relations, often relate to the show in special ways. This chapter examines these professionals' thoughts and perspectives about *Mad Men* and its portrayal of their industry. We will explore why these fans enjoy watching the show and what keeps them coming back season after season.

"Feels Right to Me"

We surveyed a group of *Mad Men* fans who work in advertising and related fields to learn about their impressions of the show. The majority worked at full-service advertising agencies. A few worked in marketing firms, digital agencies, or various companies' in-house advertising, marketing, or public-relations departments. There were also a couple of freelancers. They represented a wide range of roles from designers to strategists, creative directors to account executives, analytics directors to production managers. They had been in the business from three years to over thirty. Most had been fans of *Mad Men* since the show began and described their level of fandom as high or very high.

As we discussed in earlier chapters, *Mad Men*'s accuracy is one of the major themes that comes up repeatedly in conversations about the show. While the show's attention to detail and historical precision are often touted, as we have seen, fans continue to debate whether *Mad Men* authentically portrays its 1960s setting. Judging by the numerous publications that have been produced since the start of the show, exploring what advertising agency life was really like during the 1960s, advertising professionals also want to know whether *Mad Men*'s depictions are accurate or not. After all, just because something feels real doesn't mean it is. Yet despite their wide range of occupations, work environments, and amount of experience in the field, every one of our survey respondents agreed that *Mad Men* accurately portrayed the advertising business in the 1960s.

These advertising professionals reached their conclusions for a number of reasons. In general, they used one of three different strategies: referring to their own memories or personal experiences, relying on popular ideas of what the *Mad Men* era might have been like, and consulting with those who were there. While their backgrounds in the industry often factored into their assessments, this was not the only way these fans made their assessments.

For example, some of the respondents drew upon their personal memories of growing up in the 1960s. One respondent who owns a social-media business claimed, "Having been a child in the '60s, every detail of the show feels right to me." And another who works as a marketing and media strategist stated, "I was born in 1958. Many of the depictions reflect what I experienced growing up." This individual noted that she was about the same age as Sally during the *Mad Men* era, so watching the show progress through the 1960s makes it meaningful to her. She remembered the historical moments covered on the show, like the assassinations of President John F. Kennedy and Martin Luther King, Jr., and she appreciated the characters' different reactions to those moments. "It just [is] such an accurate — to me — reflection of what that era was. It was a turning point in society. And all that at my age between 11 and 15, that whole era was extremely impactful on me." For these individuals, then, the show feels familiar because it reminds them of their formative years in the 1960s. As a result, the respondents found those childhood memories more salient to their evaluation of *Mad Men*'s authenticity than their present-day careers in advertising, and they referenced those memories when making their judgments.

While other survey respondents also drew upon their personal experiences to assess *Mad Men*'s accuracy, they based their conclusions on their involvement in advertising in the present day. For example, one respondent told us,

"I think the main thing they capture is the working habits [of] an agency, by depicting the characters work at odd hours. Also the demands of long hours and power struggle[s] and get[ting] idea[s] noticed and climbing the ladder." For this person, who works as a designer, *Mad Men*'s 1960s setting was not important. He saw his personal experiences and observations from inside the advertising industry reflected in the working habits of the characters at the show's fictional agency, and that was enough to make *Mad Men* ring true for him.

Meanwhile, several survey participants referred to their ideas of what the 1960s might have been like, and to the progress made since, to judge the show's authenticity. In these cases respondents were relying on "popular memory" to make their assessments. As mentioned in chapter 2, Spigel used the term "popular memory" to define stories that use the past to speak to the concerns of the present. Thus, respondents who pointed to their belief that sexism, smoking, and drinking were issues in advertising in the 1960s were "engag[ing] in a kind of historical consciousness that remembers the past in order to believe in the progress of the present."

This perspective was especially clear when respondents compared the advertising business they work in today to the business as it is depicted in *Mad Men*. For example, a creative experience strategist claimed it would be "very hard to operate like [the characters in *Mad Men*] today during an era of social media and instant gratification." Another, who works as a digital account executive, pointed to the "slow creative process" depicted on the show and the reverence with which copywriters and designers with good ideas were treated as accurate to the 1960s. She indicated that the diminished presence of those things in the industry today is an improvement because creatives' egos are now less likely to get inflated to Don Draper proportions.

Finally, some respondents drew on their positions inside advertising and their access to colleagues who had been working since the *Mad Men* era in order to judge the show's accuracy. Multiple people explained that they had friends who worked in advertising during the 1960s who had confirmed that the show was true to their experiences. Other respondents who did not know anyone in advertising in the sixties said that they gleaned information about the era from other sources. For instance, a managing director of data analytics mentioned rumors he had heard about the business being "pretty out of control" during the time period as his reason for believing in the show's accuracy.

These assertions are backed up by many of the people who were actually there. For example, in a 2008 article in the *New York Times* by Alex Witchel, Jerry Della Femina, who published a bestselling book in 1970 about his early experiences in the advertising business, claimed, "*Mad Men* accurately reflects what went on. The smoking, the prejudice and the bigotry." Similarly, in a 2012 article in the *The Wire*, Jen Doll reported that Lola Cherson, who worked in PR at Grey and Davis Advertising in the late 1960s, generally approved of the show's depiction of Madison Avenue during that time. "[I]t's very good with the exception of some booboos," she said, such as Megan and Don working together after they were married and Joan showing cleavage at the office.

We were lucky enough to find our own former Mad Man, Don Potter, to talk about how the show compared to his personal experiences working on Madison Avenue during the sixties. Potter's career in advertising encompassed roles as everything from an account executive to a creative director, and he continues to consult for the industry to this day. When you talk to him, it quickly becomes clear that he loves advertising and that he loves the attention *Mad Men* has brought to the industry. He counts himself as a fan of both advertising and the show. He told us, "I watch it because I am a fan of the whole business and I think [the show is] pretty true to things."

Potter said that during the sixties there was certainly as much smoking and drinking in the industry as *Mad Men* would lead us to believe, although he was quick to point out that most of the drinking took place outside the office. Also, he asserted, "for single people like me at the time, we had a hell of a lot more sex than they portray on the show." While that's hard to imagine given the amount of sex the *Mad Men* characters have, Potter explained that sex was a natural byproduct of the sexual revolution that was in progress at the time, the pill becoming available in the early 1960s, and the social lubrication provided by the abundant drinking in the industry.

Potter also noted that there were quite a few women who worked as copywriters and in other positions in advertising at the time. Because of this, he felt *Mad Men*'s depictions of Peggy's career as a copywriter and Joan's rise to agency partner were fairly well done and reflected that reality. Even the show's lack of black characters is quite realistic, he said, because outside of a single individual here or there in low-level jobs, advertising was slow to embrace nonwhites. Because of all the ways it reflects his experiences in advertising in the 1960s, Potter feels that *Mad Men* is a very realistic show: "When I watch the show I think about how it was then. And I really compare it to what I lived and it's very real."

Yet, there are people who were in advertising during the *Mad Men* era who do not feel the show reflects their real-life experiences. For example, George Lois, a renowned art director who cofounded the agency Papert Koenig Lois in 1960, told the *New York Times*' Witchel, "When I hear *Mad Men*, it's the most irritating thing in the world to me. . . . This show gives you the impression it was all three-martini lunches. . . . We worked from 5:30 in the morning until 10 at night. We had three women copywriters. We didn't bed secretaries. It was hard, hard work and no nonsense."

Allen Rosenshine, former CEO of ad agency BBDO, concurs with Lois. In a 2014 profile in *The Day* by Rita Christopher, Rosenshine said, "In the show they start drinking at 9 o'clock and they don't stop. That is nothing like what advertising was. We'd all have been dead if that were the case. . . . There isn't a character on that show that I would want to spend time with." Gerry Rubin, the cofounder of RPA, our coauthor Cynthia's former advertising agency, also doesn't see his experiences in advertising in the 1960s reflected in *Mad Men*. In a 2010 video interview entitled "RPA's Gerry Rubin on *Mad Men* and the Honda Client," Rubin said that he believes the client roster at Leo Burnett, where he started in 1962, was very similar at the time to the client roster serviced by Don Draper and his agency colleagues. But Rubin stated that he doesn't identify with the show, noting, "*Mad Men* to me is a night-time soap opera . . . it makes good theater."

A Matter of Perspective

Of course, the disagreement between former Mad Men on the accuracy of the show makes it even harder for those who were not there during the sixties to determine what parts of the series they should believe. Ultimately, though, it may come down to a matter of perspective. For example, while both Don Potter and George Lois agree that there was more than one female copywriter in advertising at the time, they disagree on whether women's presence and status are accurately depicted on *Mad Men*. Potter sees the depiction of Peggy as authentic to the times, while Lois believes the show's portrayal of women copywriters is too narrow. How could two people agree on the facts but not on the show's interpretation of them? This disagreement speaks to the difference between facts and truth. After all, truth is subjective, facts not so much. And *Mad Men*, like any television show, is most successful with those who can find a kernel of truth in the fictional stories it tells.

Nevertheless, it's important to keep in mind that fiction is both more heightened and more limited than real life. As we explained in chapter 2, the people we meet in a story world tend to be more vivid and compelling than those we meet in real life. This is why they grab our attention and engage us emotionally. So the increased intensity of the *Mad Men* characters and the drama that surrounds them make the characters both more interesting and more exaggerated than the people we meet in real life. This doesn't mean, though, that we can't relate to them and learn something about the human experience by watching their stories.

The show focuses on specific characters like Peggy in order to draw us into her story and help us identify with her struggles. If there were more than one female copywriter featured on the show, Peggy's experiences would be divided among many different characters, making it a lot more difficult to dig into the story from her perspective and sympathize with her experiences in a man's world. Regardless of the actual number of female copywriters in advertising during the sixties, one thing's for certain — these women were breaking the glass ceiling. And that is just what *Mad Men* conveys through the character of Peggy.

As Spigel observes, "[Television's] dual status as entertainment and information places the knowledge it distributes somewhere between fiction and science, between memory and history." Because we implicitly understand that relying on a television drama like *Mad Men* as our only source of information about the world of 1960s advertising is problematic, the question of authenticity opens up a dialogue between the show and the personal and professional references to which one has access. Memory is a funny thing; it can be self-serving and selective. For the people who worked on Madison Avenue in the sixties, *Mad Men* is like a Rorschach test of sorts, revealing what they remember and what parts of the show they feel are true to their personal experiences. As Della Femina put it to Witchel: "I guess it's *Rashomon*." For our survey respondents who work in advertising today, but were not part of the industry during the *Mad Men* era, the show reveals a seductive vision of their industry's past. So while it may not be entirely real, it is real enough for them to accept it as authentic, if not completely so.

The More Things Change

As we demonstrated in chapter 3, another major topic that quickly arises when fans discuss *Mad Men* is how things have changed from the 1960s to today. Present-day advertising professionals compare the business they know now with that of the 1960s by referring to both the show and the recollections of those who worked in advertising during the *Mad Men* era. Many of the current industry insiders we surveyed pointed to a range of differences between advertising in the present and the past.

Both the marketing and media strategist and a designer contended that there is greater understanding of advertising today than there was in the 1960s. However, their focus was different. The designer concentrated on the way the Internet has impacted advertising clients in the last few decades. He commented, "I think the clients are much more knowledgeable of the industry [today]. It creates a different dynamic and work turn-arounds are quicker." This individual explained that he didn't necessarily think clients are more sophisticated now than they were in the sixties, but that "clients today have access to more information and have been better educated in the specific field of . . . advertising."

The marketing and media strategist also acknowledged the power of the Internet but focused on how it had changed the way consumers understand and interact with advertising. She explained, "Advertising is more transparent now. What goes on in the dark comes out in the light, and our society is wiser and less trusting of the media as a whole." She went on to clarify that, whereas in the 1960s people relied on advertising for information about products, today the Internet enables people to gather information from many sources. As a result, today's advertisers can't make false or dubious claims because their deceptions will be discovered, and the outcry against them will be swift and loud.

For example, in *Mad Men*'s very first episode, "Smoke Gets in Your Eyes," when Don Draper pitches the tagline "It's Toasted" to Lucky Strike, the client, Lee Garner, Jr., initially hesitates because everyone's cigarettes are toasted. Don explains, though, that consumers don't know that. In fact, the tagline works because it redirects the public's attention from the dangerous health consequences of smoking. As Don tells the client, "Everybody else's tobacco is poisonous. Lucky Strike's is toasted." It would be hard for Don to get away with that kind of thinking today though. People in the know would spread the word online that the campaign made Lucky Strikes seem special in a way that they aren't. And consumers would quickly band together to shame the company and make them acknowledge the deception of their advertising. So today advertisers can no longer control the conversation about a product, instead they must be sensitive to the cultural mood and respond accordingly.

The reliance on computers and digital tools to complete work came up as another clear difference between the present day and the 1960s. A designer explained, "With computers, I think the creative process has been devalued so a man like Don . . . might have a different struggle in this era." Citing his own experiences with clients who ask for "endless rounds of revisions," this respondent explained that computers make clients feel like requests to see additional options for campaigns are no big deal. He felt this undermines the expertise of the creative director. This advertising insider believed *Mad Men* was depicting the start of the devaluation of the creative process at the beginning of season seven when Lou Avery, the creative director who takes over at Sterling Cooper & Partners after Don's breakdown, "lacks Don's authority and creativity."

Respondents didn't always agree on whether there is less sexism, racism, and partying in the advertising business today than in the sixties or whether the industry's professionals have just gotten better at covering those things up. A female designer struck an optimistic tone, saying, "Women are pretty equal to men now. Our clothing and style of living has changed drastically. There isn't sex, alcohol, smoking or drugs inside the workplace, except the occasional beer or glass of wine after work hours." A male planning director offered a more qualified perspective, noting that advertising is now "slightly less sexist. [And] booze and drugs are slightly more hidden." And a female director of account planning similarly felt that today the industry displayed "less open chauvinism and racism. Less drugs and drinking. More concern with being politically correct."

Yet both the director of account planning and the planning director agreed that these things are still present in the industry. The planning director claimed, "Binge drinking is common at events." And the director of account planning observed that many advertising agencies have very few women and people of color at the executive level.

Mad Men facilitates comparisons between the present and the past by offering what feels like a realistic portrait of 1960s Madison Avenue. While the show feels real for any number of reasons, it is important to remember that we are only able to assess its portrait of the past from our position in the present. So while we refer to our own lives or the lives of former real-life Mad Men as a means for determining the truth of the show and deciding how things have changed since the 1960s, we also know those references are subjective and imperfect. Even as we come to conclusions about the truth of *Mad Men* and the way advertising has evolved since the era it depicts, some doubt remains. For our survey respondents, that doubt became more apparent when they turned their attention to the show's individual characters.

Character Realism

While most of our survey respondents believed the characters were an accurate reflection of the real people who worked in advertising in the 1960s, many also noted that they were stereotypes, archetypes, or exaggerations. This observation again speaks to the heightened nature of fictional stories and the characters who populate them. But, as we have explained, just because a character is an exaggeration doesn't mean she can't reveal something truthful. As Peter Osnos contended in a 2011 article in the *Atlantic*, "The [*Mad Men*] characters actually do reflect the spirit of the age in the way popular culture should, amplified for effect but not to the point of caricature. Most of the figures gradually reveal enough about their lives to humanize them within the bounds of familiar behavior rather than rendering them off-the-wall."

Ultimately most of our respondents did not dismiss the characters as completely unrealistic. The marketing and media strategist summed up this perspective: "I feel what the show's characters reflect *seems* to depict more of the *essence* of Madison Ave [in the 1960s]." At the same time, there were respondents who felt the characters are very true to life. A director in an in-house advertising department commented, "[The characters] are spot on with what I think people would have been like." Meanwhile others noted that the characters are like the people who work in advertising in the present day. For example, the creative experience strategist explained, "The construct of those characters still exist[s] today. They are just playing to a different setting." And the planning director described the characters as "stereotypes of the time period combined with what people are like in the industry today."

In fact, multiple respondents agreed that despite the fact that characters like Don aren't always depicted in the most flattering ways, there are many people in the industry who are similar to the characters. As the planning director declared, "A lot of people in advertising *are* promiscuous, drunken, sexist jerks who neglect their children. So it would be difficult to parse that out from the show." Are industry insiders concerned, then, that people will come away from *Mad Man* believing everyone in advertising is that way? For the most part, survey respondents seemed unconcerned. A designer told us, "I have not given much thought to the lingering perception of the industry as a result of the show. . . . I guess it doesn't bother me because it has not affected or influenced my life in any significant manner." And the marketing and media strategist asserted, "I think it makes it look sexy to be bad."

In contrast, Don Potter, the former Mad Man we interviewed, did not appreciate the depictions of most of the characters. His assessment, however, was focused on the professional success of the characters. He concluded that the show lacked a good person to pitch the agency's creative output to clients. This assessment included Don Draper, who, Potter said, "doesn't grab me as far as a creative guy. He doesn't make me say, 'Wow, this guy understands the consumer.'" He continued, "They're missing . . . somebody who presents the creative spark in a sparkling way." The only character Potter felt was a good representation of an ad man is Roger Sterling. Potter explained, "Roger is a Freudian delight and he'd be a fun guy to have a drink or two with. . . . He knows how to romance clients."

Relating to Situations

Potter's evaluation of the characters was based on his long experience working in advertising. And even though he doesn't always feel the characters are good examples of advertising professionals, he clearly feels the situations they find themselves in accurately depict the challenges of working in the industry. This perspective was shared by many of our survey respondents, who could relate to *Mad Men*'s portrayals of the characters' work activities and their interactions with clients.

For example, some respondents saw the difficulties, stress, and long hours that are part of their jobs reflected on the show. A designer noted, "Being on the creative side I can definitely relate to the heavy work load and last minute changes. Also, the struggle of pitching and dealing with difficult clients is still present, if not magnified." Meanwhile the director of account planning could understand "the pressure, the debate, the conflicting agendas." Another respondent explained, "I'm a designer at an agency and when I watch the show it feels like I'm at work but in the 60s! My creative space looks like their creative space, messy with inspiration, food all over, beer, coffee, pencils and paper everywhere. Then the creative process and the pitch to the client are almost identical minus the fact that everything is drawn for their creative boards. I do a lot of working all night, every night before the deadline, just like they do in the show. Except I don't smoke or have sex with my coworkers on the job." And when it came to clients, this designer also confessed that in her experience, "There is a lot of schmoozing that goes on with ad clients just like in the show. Dinner and drinks meetings. A lot of talking beforehand."

There were several respondents who felt the show's depiction of 1960s advertising as a wild culture of partying and drinking mirrored their own experiences in advertising today. The digital account executive identified with

Figure 23. Peggy and the creative team at work in the creative workspace at Sterling Cooper & Partners during season six, episode six, "Man with a Plan."

the "company parties, drinking, politics, egos, and strange shenanigans that can only happen in advertising." She commented that "[advertising's] a crazy, fun, wild industry at times," just like it can be on *Mad Men*. Meanwhile a creative director saw both the work stress and the fun associated with his job echoed on *Mad Men*: "Office politics. . . . Hack account people messing up the work. Late hours, and unrealistic timelines. And lots of partying between those times."

There were also multiple respondents who saw the tightropes they walk with their clients reflected in the client relationships depicted on the show. The creative director pointed to the parallels between his experiences with clients and those of the characters on *Mad Men*, including "account guys kissing the client ring to keep the account. Creative people trying to make moving work that will build an emotional connection with consumers." He concluded, "When art and commerce meet, it's never a harmonious relationship." This sentiment reflects both this respondent's work experience as well as the friction that many of *Mad Men*'s characters face at the office.

Clearly, advertising professionals often relate to *Mad Men* through the lens of their jobs. *Mad Men* has portrayed everything from acing the pitch to having work rejected, from getting the account to saying the wrong thing to a colleague or client, from creating successful work to losing the account, and more. In fact, because the show depicts situations that evoke memories of comparable experiences in their own work lives, *Mad Men* primes many ad people's professional identities. As a result, this part of these professionals' self-concept becomes salient as they watch *Mad Men*'s characters navigate the drama at their fictional agency. This very personal perspective influences what advertising professionals take away from the show. As a designer told us, "I do find that the sections of the show relating closest to the work and the ads are the episodes or scenes that I find most interesting. I think being in the . . . advertising field personally, they resonate most with me."

Relating to Characters

The personal way in which people currently working in advertising respond to *Mad Men*'s sixties-era advertising professionals was reflected in the way our survey respondents identified with some of the characters. While many of the respondents were skeptical about the authenticity of some of the characters, they still connected with those whose experiences mirrored their own.

As we mentioned in earlier chapters, identification is more likely with characters we see as similar to us. While that similarity can come from common demographics like age, race, or gender, it can also come from a common occupation or the ability to comprehend and empathize with a character's experiences. Most of our survey respondents were able to understand and identify with the career struggles and successes of at least one of the *Mad Men* characters because the character's professional experiences were similar to their own.

For instance, a number of respondents with varying degrees of experience in the business related to Peggy's efforts to rise through the agency ranks and gain her colleagues' respect. The director of account planning, an industry veteran of more than thirty years, explained that she identified with "[Peggy's] struggle to be seen and treated as an equal." Similarly, the creative director, who had been in the industry for eighteen years, said he related to Peggy because he too "was a creative who had to fight my way from the bottom." And a designer with eight years of experience noted, "I feel I can relate to Peggy because she has some of the same qualities I have. She is professional, determined, creative, strong-willed, confident and kind. I like watching her progress on the show." And another designer who had worked in the industry for seven years observed, "I . . . feel [Peggy] is one of the least respected figures but contributes a great deal. This is something I can personally relate to."

Survey respondents who identified with other characters also cited the ways in which those characters were like them to explain their choices. The media and marketing strategist, for example, said she related to Joan Harris because both she and Joan are "voluptuous and smart." She added, "I used . . . both [qualities] to my advantage to get ahead without sleeping to the top." Meanwhile, the managing director of data analytics identified with Harry Crane, the head of Sterling Cooper & Partners' media department and the man who pushes for the agency to get its first computer, "because it's my job to do analytics in a building where people are afraid of numbers (but love to boast that our agency uses advanced analytics)." In other words, he saw the challenges of his job paralleled in the challenges Harry Crane faces at work.

It's Personal

It's apparent, then, that one of the draws of *Mad Men* for many contemporary advertising professionals is the way it enables them to consider their own professional experiences. But many of our survey respondents also acknowledged that *Mad Men* is not exclusively about advertising. As a designer said, "I think the advertising field was a good vehicle to show the changing culture with lots of potential stories for Don and team to have exposure to cultural events and play a role in reacting to them." The marketing and media strategist concurred, noting, "Advertising is most reflective of society's emotions and passions and trends and it's a great vehicle to give you an anthropological look at what society was like at that time." And the planning director concluded, "Really I think it's a story about people, with the '60s and advertising as a hook." Yet, while they recognized advertising is only one element in a highly complex show, they also confessed that they couldn't help but watch *Mad Men* from their perspective within the industry. As the planning director explained, "[I've] watch[ed] the entire series from within the context of my life and advertising career."

Thus, *Mad Men* is personal to these advertising insiders because it speaks to their professional lives. Furthermore, the show depicts work experiences that are recognizable to them in the context of the glamorous and exciting world of 1960s Madison Avenue. This causes *Mad Men* to be not only relatable but also highly entertaining to these individuals. So, while they know the characters are imperfect representations, these advertising professionals can't help but relate to them and see their own career struggles echoed in the characters' career struggles. In other words, these professionals see enough of their work experience reflected in *Mad Men* that the show has become a source of identification and connection for them.

While it is certainly not the only reason they watch, *Mad Men* fans in advertising enjoy seeing their professional identities represented on the show. And the fact that those identities take on a period flare makes them even more alluring. As Michael Bérubé observes in his afterword in the 2013 book *Mad Men, Mad World*, "I watch the show not so much for its soap-opera aspects or for its sense of period style (both of which I enjoy in moderation) but for its willingness to take advertising seriously *while* offering a critique of the social milieu of the profession." Many of the advertising professionals who are fans of the show likely share this fascination. *Mad Men*, then, provides these fans with a vehicle through which they can contemplate the challenges, rewards, and ultimately the value of their work.

Aspiration and Inspiration

Mad Men's depictions of creative brilliance and its polished period setting have grabbed the attention of many fans, and this is also true of fans in the advertising profession. Various aspects of the show inspired many of our survey respondents. Despite real-life Mad Man Don Potter's reservations about Don Draper's abilities to understand and service clients, several of our survey respondents felt Don Draper displayed real brilliance as an ad man and confessed that they aspired to emulate him professionally.

For example, the planning director said of Don, "He's cool, he's suave,

Figure 24. Don delivering the Carousel presentation for Kodak — which one survey respondent described as "iconic" — in season one, episode thirteen, "The Wheel."

and he's the genius that we all wish we could be." Meanwhile, the media and marketing strategist acknowledged that, despite "his narcissism and lack of integrity," she still admired Don's business prowess, explaining, "As a business woman, when I get into a difficult business situation, I ask myself, 'What Would Don Draper Do?'"

So while Don Draper may not always come across as the most likeable character on *Mad Men*, the show often presents his skill for channeling his abilities into the creation of original and inventive advertising work as his most redeeming quality. Don is portrayed as someone who is able to evoke emotions through his creative work and deliver persuasive presentations, such as the powerful Carousel speech, Don's marketing pitch to Kodak for their new slide projector from the season one finale. This makes him attractive and intriguing to audiences. Advertising often gets a bad rap in our contemporary culture. But in the hands of Don Draper, advertising often seems gripping, noble, and awe-inspiring. Thus, *Mad Men*'s depiction of Don Draper's creative genius burnishes the profession's image in the eyes of the general public while providing a positive image that advertising professionals can associate themselves with and even aspire to — as some of our respondents do.

Figure 25. One survey respondent was inspired to decorate her office "*Mad Men*–esque." Photo by CLM.

Some survey respondents noted that they were either inspired by the advertising campaigns presented on the show or influenced by the show's design aesthetic. In reference to the inspiration he takes from the ad campaigns shown on *Mad Men*, one designer commented, "I think the show does a great job of finding nuggets of genius which can still work in modern advertising. The simplicity of their work creates a timeless effect which I think inspires a lot of creatives because we all have a desire to create a legendary campaign."

In addition, the media and marketing strategist stated that, for her, the show's advertising work demonstrates "the fact that the base of human nature remains consistent . . . despite [modern] external influences." She elaborated, "How the external impacts the internal [through advertising] . . . is well told in many *Mad Men* episodes and inspiring for me in my work." For one respondent, the show's sixties-era aesthetic even influenced the way she presented herself at work. She explained, "I decorated my office *Mad Men*-esque."

Gratification and Validation

On the one hand, *Mad Men* presents work situations that are recognizable and relatable to today's advertising professionals. On the other, the show helps inspire and influence the creative work, presentation styles, and business approaches of those professionals who feel that the work situations presented on the show are applicable to their own jobs.

One way to understand the show's resonance for fans in advertising and related fields is through the framework of uses and gratifications theory. This theory states that people are motivated to select and watch television and other media based on the specific wants and needs they believe a given piece of media will gratify. As we have shown, watching *Mad Men* may offer specific gratifications to advertising professionals that differ from those available to others. *Mad Men* is a critically lauded and successful show, and fans in advertising can associate the respect and admiration the show commands with their occupation and, by extension, with themselves. As a result, *Mad Men* supports advertising professionals' favorable perceptions of their occupation and their industry. Further, advertising professionals can attribute any discrepancies between their experiences in the industry and those depicted on *Mad Men* to the show's time period or its complicated characters.

Thus, fans in advertising are proud to have their profession represented by *Mad Men*. This is why one of our survey respondents told us, "My agency was mentioned in the show a few times last season." When those who currently work in advertising hear the names of agencies they recognize on the show, it gives the series greater relevance and authenticity and makes them feel a personal stake in the show—especially if they're employed at the agency mentioned. It's a thrill to hear your company or client referenced on a television show about your business. Thus, just as *Mad Men*'s period setting enables these fans to psychologically distance themselves from the social issues it depicts, such as sexism and racism, its advertising agency setting encourages them to use the show in a way that is pertinent to their lives — namely to consider their profession and their place within it.

In 2008 Matthew Weiner told Witchel of the *New York Times* that he chose to set *Mad Men* in the advertising industry because it offered a "way to talk about the image we have of ourselves, versus who we really are." But *Mad Men* also offers a means for advertising professionals to understand their work and their business. While the industry has often been disparaged and dismissed, *Mad Men* takes advertising seriously by showcasing work that is thoughtful, innovative, and inspiring. According to *Mad Men*, people who work in advertising are creative, fun, glamorous, and interesting. Thus, fans of *Mad Men* in the advertising industry can use the show as a rallying point, something that validates their professional pursuits, enhances their self-concept, and gratifies their desire to see their profession in a positive light. Regardless of the time period it depicts, *Mad Men* is an important means through which people who currently work in advertising, marketing, or public relations can think about and grapple with their profession.

Epilogue

On May 17, 2015, the *Mad Men* series finale aired. At the show's gala send-off, celebrity fans gave interviews, voicing their preferences, hopes, and interpretations of the ride they had taken with the series. American television journalist Katie Couric expressed a desire to know that her favorite characters were going to be okay. Throughout the series, some fans speculated that Don Draper would take a dive off a real building, fulfilling the promise of the show's opening animated sequence. Some fans wanted Don to take that plunge to end the frustration they felt watching him lurch uncertainly though life, and in their view, wounding those closest to him—including himself.

The finale, titled "Person to Person," has already been called ambiguous and it will certainly be evaluated and debated for years to come as *Mad Men* takes its place in television history. There is no single interpretation of the ending and no single interpretation of the show in general. Fans have different perspectives on the story, bringing pieces of their own life experiences and emotional inner lives to bear.

On Resolutions and Trade-Offs

We've considered the way sixties gender prescriptions played out in the show. From that standpoint, there was much speculation about what would come of working women Peggy and Joan, and where Betty would find herself as the last screen images faded. For these women, and arguably most of the main characters, their final trajectories represented trade-offs, each attaining something positive at the cost of losing something else of value.

In the end, we found Peggy winning Pete's respect for her work. You'll recall that Pete had declared earlier that her work was just as good as any woman's in the business. However, on his last day in the office, Pete observed that someday people would brag about having worked with Peggy.

But her success came at a cost. Across the seasons, we saw Peggy make her career the center of her world, to the detriment of her personal life. Some fans wondered if she had become too much like Don in that she gradually came to act as though people were less important than career success.

As we noted in chapter 4, Peggy was the most popular character for fan-fiction writers to write about, and their story lines often filled in the personal life some felt she lacked on the show, for example, by romantically pairing her with Ted, Stan, Pete, or even Don. When offered a partnership, we wonder if she will climb the ladder of success even faster than Pete predicted. Instead, Stan advises her that there is more to life than work and that the offer on the table did not take advantage of her true talents. When the finale aired, "Steggy" (Stan + Peggy) shippers everywhere saw their wishes granted as fanon became canon: Stan and Peggy fell into each other's arms and de-clared their love. She chooses to remain at McCann and work with him, rather than join Joan's new firm in order to have her name on the door.

As for Joan, when she met successful entrepreneur Richard, fans were hopeful that she had found lasting love. But much like the men in her past relationships, Richard only wanted Joan to cater to his plans. Instead, she chooses to start her own business, "Holloway Harris Productions" (com-prised of her maiden and married names), rather than settle for another dis-appointing man. Many fans were happy to watch Joan focus on the work she loved over another man who fell short. One fan humorously wrote, "Finally, Joan's ex-husband was good for something" because at least he provided her the second name she wanted for her company.

And what of the boys? Ken and Pete encountered some twists and turns that we didn't see coming. As mentioned in chapter 6, Ken was beloved by fans for his disdain of industry politics and equitable relationships with female colleagues. In a climactic turn, he gives up his dream of becoming a professional author. He chooses to stay in the ad business in order to exact revenge on rival Pete and on Roger for firing him. Many fans found these re-venge scenes as rewarding as Ken did, though others felt this was a sad tra-jectory for one of the show's most likable characters. It gave fans solace, however, that Ken sought out Joan as a professional colleague, reminding us why we liked him in the first place.

Meanwhile, some of our desire to punch Pete Campbell diminished, as he appeared to grow up in the final mini-season. He reconciles with his wife, Trudy, and flies his family to greener pastures. Not everyone loved seeing him get what they interpreted as the happiest ending of all in the finale. One fan lamented, "Pete gets the happy ending? Pete Freaking Campbell?" Others felt more satisfaction at watching Pete gain perspective and treat his family with more respect.

Having watched Sally grow from a little girl to a young woman, many fans wanted to feel, as they said goodbye, that she would be all right. When we learned that Betty was dying of lung cancer in the second-to-last episode (a development some fans viewed as a vital health message, while others announced their preference to watch other characters learn that particular lesson), we saw Sally step gracefully into the role of the family's rock. Fans commented that watching the young woman hold little Gene on her lap, teach Bobby how to make dinner, and comfort a distraught Henry were all poignant moments for them.

Sally seemed very grown up as she abandoned a trip to Europe to tend to the family's needs. Even though she made this sacrifice, fans felt confident that she would ultimately land on her feet. As one blogger from the website *Basket of Kisses* opined, "Sally will go to Madrid — someday." Meanwhile, there was broad appreciation for the hint of resolution to the tumultuous relationship between Betty and Sally. In a letter spelling out Betty's dying wishes, Sally learns that her mother feels that the fact that her daughter marches to the beat of her own drummer is ultimately a good thing that will help her do well in life. Many fans agree.

And what of Don Draper/Dick Whitman, the lost soul? The second half of season seven sees Don wandering. Some fans felt Don was chasing meaning on his travels. Others felt his meanderings were more along the lines of the same old cut-and-run routine that made them hate Don all along. There was even a faction who declared that they didn't care if Don lived or died, as long as he went away.

Don's journey found him finally disclosing to other war veterans that he had inadvertently killed his commanding officer in the Korean War. Their acceptance of him despite his revelation was healing. Within the same story arc, he tries to put a handsome young man on a better life path than he himself took. Many viewers saw Don's giving his car to the young man as a way for Don to "pay it forward"—a positive sign of an upward turn in Don's life.

In the finale, Don ends up at an early-seventies Esalen Institute retreat of sorts. There, in a group therapy session, he has a moment of empathy and transformation catalyzed by hearing another man describe himself as invisible to his family. In the end, the retreat's therapy and meditation seem to help Don get cleaned up and even become content (a welcome evolution of Don's earlier, negative views on therapy for fans who remember and cringe at them).

In the final moment of the series, a beatific smile lights up the meditating Don's face and we flash to the famous Hilltop Coke ad, which was actually produced in real life by McCann-Erickson (Don's new advertising firm) in 1971. Fans speculated about whether the ending implied that Don wrote that ad in a moment of meditative inspiration. Or you could view it, as Alessandra Stanley in the *New York Times* did, as the show's final wink to its audience: "Mad Men ended with a joke, and it was on us. Coca-Cola actually was the real thing." Whether it was a joke, an inspiration, or something else more subtle, the story took a conversation-starting series of twists at the end. At the very least, we can say that from women's equality to therapy and meditation, we saw some interesting people as products of their times. At the best, we can say that we loved them and that we liked where the series left them.

According to the Zeigarnik effect, we remember best that which is unfinished—and therefore alive—forever. The fan consensus seems to be that *Mad Men* gave us enough resolution to satisfy our needs, while leaving us with enough open questions to keep the characters alive in our collective conscious indefinitely. After all, the men and women of *Mad Men* weren't superheroes or drug kingpins, kings or queens, or mob bosses, they were just people like we are. We watched as they entered the next chapters of their lives as we moved on to enter ours, a bit wiser for having known them.

Bibliography

Find more on the *Mad Men Unzipped* Facebook page

To see or link to the fan works we've referenced throughout the book and for more information, check out our Facebook page: https://www.facebook.com/MadMen Unzipped.

References & Further Reading and Viewing

Adalian, J., Bernardin, M., Buchanan, K., Chianca, P., Dobbins, A., Fox., J. D., ... Vineyard, J. (2012, October 15). The 25 most devoted fan bases. *Vulture*. http://www .vulture.com/2012/10/25-most-devoted-fans.html.

Albiniak, P. (2012, January 23). Matthew Weiner: A gent, provocateur. *Broadcasting & Cable*. http://www.broadcastingcable.com/news/news-articles/matthew-weiner-gent -provocateur/112798.

Bérubé, M. (2013). Afterward: A change is gonna come, same as it ever was. In L. M. E. Goodlad, L. Kaganovsky, & R. A. Rushing (eds.), *Mad Men, mad world: Sex, politics, style, & the 1960s* (pp. 345–59). Durham, NC: Duke University Press.

Busse, K., & Hellekson, K. (2006). Introduction: Work in progress. In K. Hellekson & K. Busse (eds.), *Fan fiction and fan communities in the age of the Internet: New essays* (pp. 5–32). Jefferson, NC: McFarland.

Caddell, B. (2009). *Becoming a mad man*. http://budcaddell.com/#16.

Christopher, R. (2013, May 19). Former "Mad Men" discusses career in advertising. *The Day*. http://www.theday.com/article/20140519/ENT02/305199993.

Cohen, J. (2001). Defining identification: A theoretical look at the identification of audiences with media characters. *Mass Communication & Society, 4*(3), 245–64.

The Colbert Report. (2014, May 20). Matthew Weiner. http://thecolbertreport.cc.com /videos/zopbx2/matthew-weiner.

Coppa, F. (2006a). A brief history of media fandom. In K. Busse & K. Hellekson (eds.), *Fan fiction and fan communities in the age of the Internet: New essays* (pp. 41–59). Jefferson, NC: McFarland.

Coppa, F. (2006b). Writing bodies in space: Media fan fiction as theatrical performance. In K. Busse & K. Hellekson (eds.), *Fan fiction and fan communities in the age of the Internet: New essays* (pp. 225–44). Jefferson, NC: McFarland.

Corrigan, J. M., & Corrigan, M. (2012). Disrupting flow: *Seinfeld*, *Sopranos* series finale, and the aesthetic of anxiety. *Television & New Media*, *13*(2), 91–102. doi: 10.1177/1527476410392804.

The Daily Beast. (2014, May 11). TV's best and worst moms: "Veep," "Game of Thrones," and more. http://www.thedailybeast.com/articles/2009/05/09/marge -simpson-and-dina-lohan-the-best-and-worst-tv-moms.html.

Dill-Shackleford, K. E. (2016). *How fantasy becomes reality: Information and entertainment media in everyday life* (2nd ed.). New York: Oxford University Press.

Dill-Shackleford, K. E., Hopper-Losenicky, K., Vinney, C., Swain, L. F., & Hogg, J. L. (2015). *Mad Men* fans speak via social media: What fan voices reveal about the social construction of reality via dramatic fiction. *Journal of Fandom Studies*.

Doll, J. (2012, April 9). Reviewing the "Mad Men" world by someone who was there. *The Wire*. http://www.thewire.com/entertainment/2012/04/reviewing-mad-men -world-someone-who-was-there/50851/#disqus_thread.

Elliott, S. (2008, June 23). Madison Avenue likes what it sees in the mirror. *New York Times*. http://www.nytimes.com/2008/06/23/business/media/23adcol.html?_r=0.

FFN Research. (2011, March 18). Fan fiction demographics in 2010: Age, sex, country. http://ffnresearch.blogspot.co.uk/2011/03/fan-fiction-demographics-in-2010-age .html.

Goux, J. (2013, May 10). The 10 worst TV moms in the world: Betty Draper—*Mad Men*. *Huffington Post*. http://www.huffingtonpost.com/hulucom/the-10-worst-tv -moms-in-t_b_3248980.html.

Hinckley, D. (2014, August 22). Emmys 2014: From "Mad Men" to "Breaking Bad," the top 10 dramas of all time. *New York Daily News*. http://www.nydailynews.com /entertainment/tv/breaking-bad-game-thrones-rank-time-best-dramas-list-article -1.1912409.

Horton, D., & Wohl, R. R. (1956). Mass communication and parasocial interaction: Observations on intimacy at a distance. *Psychiatry*, *19*, 215–29.

Igartua, J. J., & Paez, D. (1998). Validity and reliability of empathy and identification with characters scale. *Psicothema*, *10*(2), 423–36.

Isakson, P. (2008, November 16). Confessions of a (fake) mad man. http://paulisakson .typepad.com/planning/2008/11/don_draper-twitter.html.

Isbouts, J. P., & Ohler, J. (2013). Storytelling and media: Narrative models from Aristotle to augmented reality. In K. E. Dill (ed.), *The Oxford handbook of media psychology* (pp. 13–42). New York: Oxford University Press. doi: 10.1093/oxford hb/9780195398809.013.0002.

Jenkins, H. (1992). *Textual poachers: Television fans and participatory culture*. New York: Routledge.

Jenkins, H. (2007, March 22). Transmedia storytelling 101. *Confessions of an Aca-Fan: The Official Weblog of Henry Jenkins.* http://henryjenkins.org/2007/03/transmedia_storytelling_101.html.

Jenkins, H. (2008). *Convergence culture: Where old and new media collide.* New York: New York University Press.

Jenkins, H. (2009, January 26). Going "mad": Creating fan fiction 140 characters at a time. *Confessions of an Aca-Fan: The Official Weblog of Henry Jenkins.* http://henryjenkins.org/2009/01/mad_men_twitter_and_the_future_1.html.

Jenkins, H. (2012). Superpowered fans: The many worlds of San Diego's Comic-Con. *Boom: A Journal of California, 2*(2), 23–36. doi:10.1525/boom.2012.2.2.22.22.

Jenkins, H., Ford, S., & Green, J. (2013). *Spreadable media: Creating value and meaning in a networked culture.* New York: New York University Press.

Keveney, B. (2012, March 26). Jessica Paré gets the world humming "Zou Bisou Bisou." *USA Today.* http://usatoday30.usatoday.com/life/television/news/story/2012-03-26/mad-men-jessica-pare/53791528/1.

Konijn, E. A., & Hoorn, J. F. (2005). Some like it bad: Testing a model for perceiving and experiencing fictional characters. *Media Psychology, 7*(2), 107–44.

Krakowiak, K. M., & Tsay-Vogel, M. (2013). What makes characters' bad behaviors acceptable? The effects of character motivation and outcome on perceptions, character liking, and moral disengagement. *Mass Communication and Society, 16*(2), 179–99.

Labrecque, J. (2014, May 19). *Mad Men* recap: Don wants to be chairman of the board. *Entertainment Weekly.* http://www.ew.com/recap/mad-men-strategy.

Lulu. (2013, October 5). AO3 census: Masterpost. *The Slow Dance of the Infinite Stars.* http://centrumlumina.tumblr.com/post/63208278796/ao3-census-masterpost.

Mad Men. (n.d.). Wikipedia. http://en.wikipedia.org/wiki/Mad_Men.

Mad Men: The inevitable alignment chart. (2010, December 6). Mightygodking.com. http://mightygodking.com/2010/12/06/mad-men-the-inevitable-alignment-chart/.

Minkel, M. (2014, October 17). Why it doesn't matter what Benedict Cumberbatch thinks of Sherlock fan fiction. *New Statesman.* http://www.newstatesman.com/culture/2014/10/why-it-doesn-t-matter-what-benedict-cumberbatch-thinks-sherlock-fan-fiction.

Osnos, P. (2011, February 22). In defense of "Mad Men." *Atlantic.* http://www.theatlantic.com/entertainment/archive/2011/02/in-defense-of-mad-men/71549/2/.

Paskin, W., & Stebner, B. (2010, July 21). Watch Betty Draper's guide to parenting. *Vulture.* http://www.vulture.com/2010/07/mad_mens_betty_drapers_guide_t.html.

rachelgoldenberg (Producer). (2014, August 6). Modern office with Christina Hendricks. http://www.funnyordie.com/videos/df522cada0/modern-office-w-christina-hendricks.

Rawling, N. (2012). *Mad Men* stuck in your head: Jessica Paré, who plays Megan Draper, talks "Zou Bisou Bisou." *Time*. http://entertainment.time.com/2012/03 /26/mad-men-stuck-in-your-head/.

Rose, F. (2012). *The art of immersion*. New York: W. W. Norton.

Rose, L. (2012, June 6a). "Mad Men" creator Matthew Weiner on Joan's water-cooler moment: "It really happened. A lot." *Hollywood Reporter*. http://www.hollywood reporter.com/news/mad-men-matthew-weiner-joan-christina-hendricks-333659.

Rose, L. (2012, June 6b). The arc of Joan. *Hollywood Reporter*. http://www.hollywood reporter.com/news/mad-men-christina-hendricks-joan-holloway-333656.

Rowles, D. (2014, January 7). The 50 best TV series on Netflix, ranked. *Uproxx*. http:// uproxx.com/tv/2015/01/the-50-best-tv-series-on-netflix-ranked/.

RPA Advertising. (2010, Sept. 7). RPA's Gerry Rubin on *Mad Men* and the Honda client [video]. https://www.youtube.com/watch?v=9w-FMXSoCKA.

Saraiya, S. (2012, March 22). Ranked: Don Draper's relationships on *Mad Men*, from most to least dysfunctional. *Nerve*. http://www.nerve.com/entertainment/ranked /ranked-don-drapers-relationships-on-mad-men-from-most-to-least-dysfunctional.

Spigel, L. (1995). From the dark ages to the golden age: Women's memories and television reruns. *Screen, 36*(1), 16–33.

Stanley, A. (2015, May 18). Shifting from *Mad Men* to strong women in series finale. *New York Times*. http://www.nytimes.com/2015/05/19/arts/television/shifting -from-mad-men-to-strong-women-in-a-series-finale.html?_r=0

Stein, L., & Busse, K. (2009). Limit play: Fan authorship between source text, intertext, and context. *Popular Communication: The International Journal of Media and Culture, 7*(4), 192–207. doi: 10.1080/15405700903177545.

Watkins, G. (2013, June 18). The *Mad Men* GQ+A: Vincent Kartheiser on whether Pete Campbell is gay. *GQ*. http://www.gq.com/blogs/the-feed/2013/06/mad-men -interview-vincent-kartheiser-pete-campbell.html.

Watkins, G. (2014, May 29). The complete quips of *Mad Men*'s Roger Sterling. *Vulture*. http://www.vulture.com/2013/04/mad-men-complete-quips-of-roger-sterling.html.

Webb, L. M., Hayes, M. T., Chang, H. C., & Smith, M. M. (2012). Taking the audience perspective: Online fan commentary about the brides of *Mad Men* and their weddings. In A. A. Ruggerio (ed.), *Media depictions of brides, wives and mothers* (pp. 223–35). Lanham, MD: Lexington Books.

What are the overarching themes of *Mad Men*? (n.d.). Retrieved from Quora: http:// www.quora.com/What-are-the-overarching-themes-of-Mad-Men.

Witchel, A. (2008, June 22). "Mad Men" has its moment. *New York Times*. http://www .nytimes.com/2008/06/22/magazine/22madmen-t.html?pagewanted=all&module =Search&mabReward=relbias%3Ar.

Writers Guild of America, West. (n.d.). 101 best written TV series. http://www.wga.org/content/default.aspx?id=4925.

Yuan, J. (2012, May 20). *Mad Men*'s Matt Weiner on how he found the perfect Megan Draper. *Vulture*. http://www.vulture.com/2012/05/mad-mens-matt-weiner-on-jessica-pare.html.

Zimmerman, A. (2014, April 13). Every woman Don Draper's hooked up with on "Mad Men." *The Daily Beast*. http://www.thedailybeast.com/articles/2014/04/13/every-woman-don-draper-s-hooked-up-with-on-mad-men.html.

Index